The New Testament Image of the Ministry

W. T. PURKISER

BEACON HILL PRESS OF KANSAS CITY
Kansas City
Missouri

The New Testament IMAGE of the MINISTRY

Second Printing, 1969

Printed in the
United States of America

ISBN: 083-410-5098

Preface

This volume had its birth in the author's desire to make a personal survey of New Testament teaching about the Christian ministry. While many modern writers have been consulted, it has been for the illustration they might give to the scripture in the way of current application. It goes without saying that the only authors who are quoted with full endorsement of all they have written are the inspired authors of the biblical books.

Portions of the following material have been presented at district preachers' meetings on the Pittsburgh, Tennessee, Maine, Houston, Northwest, and San Antonio districts of the Church of the Nazarene. Most of it was given at the Pasadena College Ministers' Workshop in June, 1967.

The author desires only that its wider circulation may help to deepen and enrich our understanding of the dignity and challenge of the ministry in today's world.

—W. T. PURKISER

Acknowledgments

Acknowledgment is gratefully given for permission to quote from copyrighted sources as follows:

The Abingdon Press: Thomas J. Mullen, *The Renewal of the Ministry.*

Charles T. Branford Co.: Th. C. Vriezen, *An Outline of Old Testament Theology.*

Channel Press: Paul R. Clifford, *The Pastoral Calling;* and Wayne C. Oates, ed., *The Minister's Own Mental Health.*

The Christian: Charles F. Kemp, "On the Work of a Pastor."

Fortress Press: H. Grady Davis, *Design for Preaching.*

Harper and Row: Gene Bartlett, *The Audacity of Preaching;* D. Elton Trueblood, *The Incendiary Fellowship;* and Kyle M. Yates, *Preaching from the Prophets.*

Light and Life Press: J. Paul Taylor, *Holiness, the Finished Foundation.*

The Macmillan Co.: D. R. Davies, *On to Orthodoxy.*

Oxford University Press: Leslie J. Tizard, *Preaching*: *The Art of Communication.*

The Westminster Press: William Barclay, *Fishers of Men;* Walther Eichrodt, *Theology of the Old Testament,* Vol. I; and Wayne C. Oates, *Protestant Pastoral Counseling.*

Contents

CHAPTER 1

The Changing Image

One of the most striking features of modern society is its rapidly changing concept of the ministry of the gospel. In no other period since the Reformation has the popular appraisal of the work of the minister altered so drastically as in the last half-century.

In a not-too-remote day, the parson would have been one of the best educated men in the community. He would have been regarded as a prime molder of public opinion. His counsel would have been sought in matters of community welfare. While his remuneration would not have been excessive, it would have compared favorably with the incomes of other professional men when provision of manse or parsonage was taken into consideration. He would have been regarded as representative of one of the most highly honored professions.

But such a day, by and large, is with us no more.

I

The signs of the shifting scene are many and varied. Not the least significant is the portrayal of the minister in literature. The 1959 survey by Horton Davies in

A Mirror of the Ministry in Modern Novels[1] reveals a preponderance of unfavorable appraisal, particularly of the Protestant preacher. Included in this category would be Nathaniel Hawthorne's selection of the Reverend Mr. Dimmesdale as the subject of slow disintegration through hypocrisy and cowardice in *The Scarlet Letter;* Elmer Gantry, the arch-hypocrite of Sinclair Lewis' bitter novel of the same name; and the caricatures of missionary and minister by W. Somerset Maugham in *Rain* and *Of Human Bondage.*

In this same general category is the cynicism of James Michener's *Hawaii.* The motion picture version of *Hawaii,* according to *Time*'s editorial writer, is the picture of

> how God-fearing but life-hating missionaries destroyed the warm brown souls they came to save. The hero is a prune-faced New England parson insuperably identified with deity. Blankly unable to perceive that the islanders are more Christian than the Christians, this religious imperialist with ruthless righteousness throws down their god of love and raises up in its stead a god of wrath. With their religion in ruins, the Hawaiians lie open to all the blessings of civilization: whisky, syphilis and economic exploitation. By film's end the native nation in only 50 years has withered from 400,000 to 150,000 souls, and the parson is forced to assume the white man's burden of guilt.[2]

In fairness to Mr. Michener it probably should be said that the portrayal of Hawaii's natives as "more Christian than the Christians" is either one of Hollywood's touches or the misconception of *Time*'s writer. It is not quite so evident in the book, although in truth the missionaries are placed in the worst possible light. One is not long in the Islands even now until he is

[1]New York: Oxford University Press, 1959.

[2]*Time,* Vol. 88, No. 16 (October 21, 1966), p. 118.

made aware of the popular judgment, "The missionaries came to do good, and they did right well"—this, of course, in view of the large real-estate holdings some of their descendants have amassed.

That even unsympathetic criticism may "play the Socratic role of gadfly"[3] will not be denied. What is relevant is the evidence from literature that the image of the ministry in our day has, to say the least, been greatly blurred.

II

Christianity Today recently reported a scientific sampling by Lou Harris and Associates purporting to show "that clergymen are down in public esteem and confidence to a rating below that of doctors, bankers, scientists, military leaders, educators, corporation heads, psychiatrists, and even local retailers. Their rating of 45 per cent, in contrast to 74 per cent for doctors, 66 per cent for scientists, 62 per cent for educators, and 57 per cent for psychiatrists, as reported by *Newsweek,* suggests disturbing things about the direction in which Americans are turning for a solution to human problems. The clergy ran a scant 1 per cent ahead of congressmen and federal government leaders."[4]

The last comparison may serve to bring to mind the peccadillos of Rev. Adam Clayton Powell, Jr., a clergyman whose ordination is recognized by the American Baptist Convention, and whose exhortations to "keep the faith, Baby" have scarcely brought dignity and honor to the ministry.

A United Press International dispatch out of New York for May 25, 1967, carries an article by Delos Smith

[3]Davies, *op. cit.,* p. 8.

[4]Vol. XI, No. 8 (January 20, 1967), p. 25.

concerning statistics from the first large-scale scientific study of public views on mental health. Smith reports, "According to a 1955 survey, 52 per cent of those asked would go first to a clergyman if they themselves had a mental or 'emotional' problem, and 18 per cent would consult a psychiatrist. The new survey found that 51 per cent of New Yorkers would choose a psychiatrist and only 4 per cent a clergyman."[5]

Thomas J. Mullen in *The Renewal of the Ministry* writes: "One of the hard facts which ministers in every denomination must face is that today a large number of people are suspicious of the preacher's motives. There is a growing attitude of anti-clericalism in America today, and not all those who share it are angry young (or old) men. . . . There may have been a time when the typical pastor was a symbol of deep dedication, self-sacrifice, and hardworking humility. However, that image is held by fewer people today than in the past."[6]

Mr. Mullen again comments: "The image of the physician or the lawyer or the teacher or the research chemist is sharp and clear. The image of a Protestant pastor between Monday and Saturday is fuzzy and confused. . . . Instead of being a voice crying in the wilderness, the Protestant ministry has demonstrated itself to be a whisper lost in the wind."[7]

One statistically measurable effect of these widely diffused attitudes is becoming apparent. It is the declining number of candidates for the ministry presenting themselves to their denominations.

[5]Jack Elinson, Elona Padilla, Marvin E. Perkins, *Public Image of Mental Health Services,* as reported in the Medford, Ore., *Mail Tribune,* May 26, 1967.

[6](New York: Abingdon Press, 1963), p. 110.

[7]*Ibid.,* pp. 20, 33.

Elton Trueblood notes:

> There is no escape from the conclusion that the professional ministry is not as attractive as it once was, and that it is difficult to attract the ablest men. There is no real chance of Church Renewal unless this problem is solved. . . . More and more the problem is that of image. The professional ministers, especially when they are persons of outstanding integrity, as many are, simply cannot accept the mold into which they are supposed to be cast. . . .
>
> Because the recruitment of the strongest leaders is absolutely necessary for the effectiveness of the Church in the contemporary world, the urgent task is that of producing a new image of religious leadership which will be sufficient to enlist the interest of such men. Unless the image of expectation is altered, we must expect further decline and even decay."[8]

Martin Marty reported the results of interviews with presidents and academic deans of a number of leading seminaries concerning the lack of adequate numbers of ministerial candidates. He found these men saying that underlying the whole problem is the fact that "the image of the ministry is obscured, diffuse, undramatic, purposeless. In the eyes of the coming generation the task of the minister is ill defined. Collegians . . . tend to view the minister as a competitive institutionalist, grabbing at whatever attention he can get in his community, concerned with budgetary needs, presenting a false front to the world and to other churches, ministering to the most traditional and defensive and uncreative element in the community."[9]

III

What might be called the external image of the ministry, with which we have largely been dealing, is

[8]*The Incendiary Fellowship* (N.Y.: Harper and Row, 1967), pp. 37-38.

[9]Quoted; Mullen, *op. cit.*, p. 35 .

probably less significant than the confusion within the Church relative to the role of the minister in today's world.

Bishop Gerald Kennedy recalls the old Scottish lady who referred to a young man of her acquaintance as obviously fitted for the ministry because he was "a right harmless laddie."[10] And Bishop Goodwin Hudson described some preachers as "mild-mannered men standing before a mild-mannered congregation, asking them to become more mild,"[11] while another spoke of "bland leaders of the bland."

Preachers are cynically said to be too busy looking for the lost coin to be out looking for the lost sheep.[12] The late A. W. Tozer referred to "the popular image of the man of God as a smiling, congenial, asexual religious mascot whose handshake is always soft and whose head is always bobbing in the perpetual Yes of universal acquiescence." This, Dr. Tozer commented with feeling, "is not the image found in the Scriptures of truth."[13]

When the virile prophetic note goes out of preaching; when, as Bishop Kennedy remarked, "the sermon never goes deeper than the silly moralisms of a religious columnist"; when the minister becomes a mechanic tinkering incessantly with ecclesiastical machinery, then "the congregation becomes a fellowship of mediocrity whose religious insights and understanding remain on the level of the kindergarten."[14]

[10]*For Preachers and Other Sinners* (New York: Harper and Row, 1964), p. 37.

[11]At the World Congress on Evangelism, Nov. 2, 1966.

[12]Quoted, editorial, *Vital Christianity,* Vol. 86, No. 38 (September 18, 1966), p. 16.

[13]*Man: The Dwelling Place of God* (Harrisburg, Pa.: Christian Publications, 1966), pp. 167-68.

[14]*Op. cit.,* p. 44.

IV

In part, the deteriorating image of the ministry both outside the Church and among its laity may very well be due to the fact that ministers themselves often betray a profound lack of understanding of their calling. The fuzziness of the image reflects the minister's own groping for an identity in modern society. Mullen makes this point: "The inadequacy of their own self-image of the ministry has been a contributing factor to the distortion of society's image of it. Every man or woman who enters the ministry must know who he is, what his motivations are, what he actually thinks of his fellow-man, and what his special temptations are."[15]

The reason for some attrition from the active ministry is no doubt suggested by the statement of James W. Burns, written as president of the International Convention of Christian Churches (Disciples of Christ): "I have had wide correspondence with all those leaving the ministry of our people since January 1, 1962. A few left their ministry because their health failed, but most of them left because their love of God was not strong enough to motivate them for the actual hard work of the ministry. The letters reveal the record of undisciplined, inadequate affection for God."[16] These are the kind of men Bishop Scanlon of the Evangelical Congregational church addressed from a text of Paul, "Quit you like men," which he reversed to become, "Men like you quit!"

But is it not at least possible that some of the failing affection for God is the result of an inadequate conception of what His call embraces? May it not be

[15]*Op. cit.*, pp. 117-18.

[16]In G. Paul Butler, editor, *Best Sermons*, Protestant edition (Princeton, N.J.: D. Van Nostrand Company, Inc., 1964), IX, 198.

that the fires of the spiritual life tend to die when deprived of the fuel that comes from an investment of life in something clearly seen to be inherently worthwhile? When the shepherd is reduced to the position of a sheep dog (or worse yet, a pet lamb!), and the fisherman becomes the keeper of an aquarium, the heart goes out of the whole ministerial enterprise.

The uncertainty of the minister as to his role is a recurrent theme in present-day writing about the profession. In his 1961 Lyman Beecher Lectures at Yale Divinity School, published as *The Audacity of Preaching,* Gene Bartlett asks, "In what relationship then does the preacher find his true identity? With what is he identified which gives him his distinction in calling and claim? This seems to be our perplexity. Carl Sandburg tells of the chameleon who got along very well adjusting moment by moment to his environment until one day he had to cross a Scotch plaid. It is related that he died at the crossroads, heroically trying to relate to everything at once!"[17]

Elton Trueblood recently wrote: "The central problem which faces the minister is that of his own identity. It is hard for him, in the midst of competing and very contradictory pressures, to know who he is. This basic problem must be solved before lesser problems can be rightly stated. Is he prophet, teacher, promoter, performer, preacher, counselor, visitor, business manager, or what?"[18]

Although in a far different realm, the preacher's problem is not unlike that of Willie Loman, the little Brooklyn salesman in Arthur Miller's portrayal of the pathetic *Death of a Salesman.* Loman's son Biff summed

[17] (New York: Harper and Brothers, 1962), p. 20.

[18] Introduction to Mullen, *op. cit.,* p. 8.

up his father's mixed-up life in six sad words: "He never knew who he was."[19]

Dr. Maxwell Maltz may be at least half right in his book on *Psycho-Cybernetics* when he points out that a negative or defective self-image may mean failure in the highest endeavors of life. I am not so sure that the positive side of his thesis is as valid as its negative side. But certainly one's self-image is important in its limiting if not in its liberating effects.[20]

In many cases the varied demands of the minister's calling are real and cannot easily be waved aside. With a little more than tongue in cheek, Methodist Minister Pierce Harris wrote, "The modern preacher has to make as many visits as a country doctor, shake as many hands as a politician, prepare as many briefs as a lawyer, and see as many people as a specialist. He has to be as good an executive as the president of a university, as good a financier as a bank president, and in the midst of it all, he has to be so good a diplomat that he could umpire a baseball game between the Knights of Columbus and the Ku Klux Klan."[21]

Some of the competing and almost contradictory roles the preacher is called upon to assume in our day arise from the restructuring life of the Church under the conditions of modern society. Illustrative of this is the marked population shift from rural to urban centers, the growth of "surburbia" and the contrasting "inner city," the dislocation and relocation of vast numbers of

[19]Cited by C. William Fisher, *Evangelistic Moods, Methods, and Messages* (Kansas City, Mo.: Beacon Hill Press of Kansas City, 1967), p. 115.

[20]*Psycho-Cybernetics* (New York: Prentice-Hall, Inc., 1960).

[21]Quoted by H. C. Brown, Jr., in A. W. Blackwood, ed., *Special-Day Sermons for Evangelicals* (Great Neck, N.Y.: Channel Press, Inc., 1961), pp. 396-97.

people in an increasingly heterogeneous mass. The simple structures of parish life have been replaced by the complexities of a mobile society whose "neighborhood" is not defined in city blocks as much as in vocational or professional associations.

To the extent that new ministerial roles represent new ways of doing the old task, they are all to the good. To the extent to which they represent the introduction of extraneous or incidental functions, they cannot fail to be detrimental and dangerous.

V

All of this but heightens the importance of our theme. Image may indeed be an overworked term, and excessive concern with it may become unhealthy, as Foy Valentine suggested when he wrote: "There is . . . a certain preoccupation with 'image' among us which indicates we are not so concerned about who and what we really are before God Almighty as we are about what people think of us."[22] Yet a proper conception of the work of the ministry is but the more necessary since the popular conception is so confused and so inadequate. Abraham Lincoln's oft-quoted words are relevant: "If we could first know where we are, and whither we are tending, we could better judge what to do, and how to do it."

Image is broadly defined as "a mental conception . . . symbolic of a basic attitude and orientation."[23] It may range all the way from a more or less apt metaphor to what is identified as the basic element in all knowl-

[22]*The Cross in the Marketplace* (Waco, Tex.: Word Books, 1966), p. 51.

[23]Webster's *Third International Dictionary, ad loc.*

edge.[24] The image functions as a tool to describe and convey impressions. It provides a mode of perceiving a given reality especially where not amenable to objective visibility or measurement. It serves to advance self-understanding, integration, and a sense of direction.[25]

When we turn from the welter of confusion that marks human appraisals of the ministry to the pages of the New Testament, we find diversity without discrepancy, variety without uncertainty. The variety is great. In fact, the question might well be raised whether we have an image, or images, of the minister in the Bible. Many metaphors and descriptive terms are used. But there is a very real sense in which the diverse images coalesce into a sort of composite portrait. It is for this that we shall seek in the chapters that follow.

Some of the groundwork has already been done in *The Preacher's Portrait,* by John R. W. Stott, albeit from a different perspective. Mr. Stott's prefatory words are descriptive of our task: "We need, I believe, to gain in the Church today a clearer view of God's revealed ideal for the preacher, what he is and how he is to do his work. . . . This, I suggest, is *the preacher's portrait,* a portrait painted by the hand of God Himself on the broad canvas of the New Testament."[26]

[24]As per Kenneth E. Boulding, *The Image: Knowledge in Life and Society* (Ann Arbor: The University of Michigan Press, 1956).

[25]The latter three points, made by Paul S. Minear with regard to images of the Church, are relevant to the image of the ministry; cf. *Images of the Church in the New Testament* (Philadelphia: The Westminster Press, 1960), pp. 22-24.

[26](Grand Rapids, Mich.: Wm. B. Eerdmans Publishing Company, 1961), p. 7. The 1961 Payton Lectures at Fuller Theological Seminary, Pasadena, Calif.

VI

Before filling in some of the wealth of detail to be found in the Scriptures, it would be helpful to sketch the broad outlines of the emerging picture. There are certain basic characterizations of the ministry that underlie and find expression in all the concrete imagery of the New Testament.

First, the ministry is *a calling*. As of the Old Testament priesthood, it must be said of the New Testament minister, "No man taketh this honour unto himself, but he that is called of God, as was Aaron" (Heb. 5:4). Describe it as one will, there is a "Woe is unto me, if I preach not the gospel!" (I Cor. 9:16) in the consciousness of every true man of God.

Paul R. Clifford expressed it thus in *The Pastoral Calling*:

> Before any man is ordained to the Christian ministry or inducted into the pastorate of any church, he should have had an experience of inward constraint, interpreted as the call of God through the Spirit to the work of the ministry. No church can give this call; it can only recognize that someone has it. In other words, a man may have an authority which is in no way derived from his fellows, but comes directly from God. Closely allied to this is the minister's awareness of the authority of the gospel he is commissioned to proclaim. Because it is *God's* word, rooted and grounded in His mighty acts of creation and redemption, it is not within human control. Men may bear witness to it; they cannot invent it or change it. It is on the ultimate authority of God and the derivative authority of His word in the Scriptures that the authority of a minister's own calling rests.[27]

Much has been written about the nature of the call to the ministry. It comes, as do all God's movings, in a

[27] (Great Neck, N.Y.: The Channel Press, 1961), p. 26.

variety of ways. It is an inner constraint, a sense that this is destiny, always compelling but usually growing stronger with the years. As an unnamed poet described it in the experience of Matthew:

> *I heard Him call, "Come, follow,"*
> *That was all;*
> *My goal grew dim,*
> *My heart went after Him;*
> *I arose and followed,*
> *That was all;*
> *Who would not follow*
> *If he heard Him call?*[28]

Second, the ministry is *a covenant*. Perhaps this has best been put by Gene Bartlett in two paragraphs from *The Audacity of Preaching*:

> God does not require what He will not offer. It is, in short, a covenant, God's offering of Himself as well as His requiring obedience of us. So the sufficiency was never meant to be in us alone but only in Him. The call to the ministry is the call to a *covenant.* The importance of that truth is almost beyond measure. Paul caught it in those early chapters of II Corinthians which deal with the ministry of the new covenant. That covenant is still the only answer to our alarm. Those chapters of II Corinthians are filled with assurance and hope, the summary of it found in the moving words of the sixth verse of the third chapter, "Our sufficiency is of God, who has qualified us to be ministers of a new covenant." That is still the only ground of our qualification. This means quite simply that the ministry in any of its expressions is a tremendous act of faith—nothing less than that! It is a mighty act of trust which goes about this audacious business of ministry, believing where we cannot prove, but taking God's word for it.

[28]Quoted by George K. Bowers, *God Here and Now* (Anderson, Ind.: The Warner Press, 1961), p. 65.

> Before we have placed undue blame upon the contemporary culture for the maceration of the minister, let us see what it can mean to quit fleeing from the full claim, and to turn at last and put our trust in this word. Then we yet may be "qualified to be ministers of a new covenant." Perhaps we shall be no less active in our ministry, but it will be the activity of assurance, not that of anxiety. We even may do many of the same things which mark the pastorate today, but they will be meaningful, taking on a new sacramental nature. At least we shall be able to bring a whole man to the proclaiming of the whole gospel.[29]

It is the covenant that guarantees, as Dr. R. T. Williams used to say so often, "not success, but the possibility of success." It is confidence in the promises of a God who keeps covenant with His people that sustains in the dormant and fallow times. Adoniram Judson is often quoted as proclaiming the future to be as bright as the promises of God. What is not always remembered is that this statement was made before any breakthrough came for the gospel in Burma, in the midst of long years of labor without so much as a single convert to show for it.

We need to see more than almost anything else that, though we plant and water, God gives the increase. We are not building our church. Christ is building His Church through us. Such a conception will not make us less active. It will fortify our activity with assurance, not frustrate it with anxiety. To us as to His original band that He called and with which He covenanted, Christ addresses the words: "Fear not, little flock, for it is your Father's good pleasure to give you the kingdom" (Luke 12:32).

Third, the ministry is *a commitment*, a choice. This relates to an essential aspect of the biblical concept of

[29]*Op. cit.*, pp. 134-35.

covenant. The covenant always originates with God. The initiative is His. But it requires the choice, the commitment, of those to whom it is offered. Someone has told the story of an eccentric old man whose delight was in tall tales from his past—like the time he drove "a flock of bees from Utah to California, and never lost a bee." He is pictured as receiving his government pension check, which he would wave before all beholders. "See those signatures—the comptroller general, and the treasurer of the United States. See that picture —the picture of Washington. Yet it isn't worth a red cent until I sign it." The truth is, of course, he was right.

Call and covenant find completion only in choice, commitment to the purposes of God. For some of us, that commitment has not been without struggle. George Adam Smith wrote with regard to Isaiah, "It is strange, and yet it is not strange, that the great prophets shrank at first from their task. A too great readiness to plunge into the awful work is a sure sign of a shallow soul—of a soul that has not measured its own weakness, the greatness of its task, or the majesty of its God."[30]

Fourth, the ministry is *a commission.* This is the Church's part. Since the Holy Spirit first spoke to the church at Antioch and said, "Separate unto me Barnabas and Saul for the work whereunto I have called them" (Acts 13:2), and the church responded by laying hands upon them and sending them away, the credentials of minister and missionary have been recognized as coming from the church. The church cannot convey the call. The church must confirm the call by recognizing the gifts and graces already imparted. Whatever it be named

[30]"Isaiah," Vol. I, *The Speaker's Bible,* edited by Edward Hastings (Aberdeen, Scotland: "The Speaker's Bible" Office, 1934), p. 49.

—license, ordination, commission, induction—the church sets its seal upon those who will minister to or for it.

When next you view or participate in an ordination service, note well the words used: "a minister of the gospel in the church." We are not ordained as ministers *of* the church. We are ordained as ministers of the gospel *in* the church. Yet we are ministers in the church which, for most of us, was before us, and which will be after we are gone.

This has some sweeping implications for the preacher in relation to the content of his preaching. He is speaking the church's faith to the world, not his own vagaries and private interpretations. We can well listen to Peter Forsyth at this point:

> The minister of a Church in its pulpit is not a free lance (I say in *its* pulpit, not in *his*). He is not a mere preaching friar, a vagrant Evangelist, gathering his audience in streets and lanes, hedges and highways, as he can find them. He enters on a position of trust which he did not create. He is licensed to it when he is called by its custodian, the Church. Any call to a minister is, in substance, a license conferred on him, however much in form it may be a petition addressed to him. He stands on a platform, an institution, which is provided for him, and he owes practical regard to the Church which provides it. He bespeaks men's attention, not in virtue of his personal quality merely, but in virtue of a charge and Gospel, given both to minister and Church, which both must serve. He is not free to vend in his pulpit the extravagances of an eccentric individualism, nor the thin heresies of the amateur. He is not entitled to ask men to hear with respectful silence the freaks of mere mother-wit, or the guesses of an untutored intelligence. When a man is entrusted with the pastoral care of a Church from its pulpit, he accepts, along with the normality of Scripture, the obligations, limitations, and reserves of the pastoral commission.[31]

[31]*Positive Preaching and the Modern Mind* (New York: George H. Doran Company, 1907), p. 101.

Fifth, the ministry is *a consecration*—here used in its original meaning, not as man's offering, but as God's act of setting apart for sacred ends. This is a valid, though not often recognized, application of the term. It finds its chief popular illustration in Fanny Crosby's correctly phrased lines:

Consecrate me now to Thy service, Lord,
By the power of grace divine;
Let my soul look up with a steadfast hope,
And my will be lost in Thine.

Missionary Geraldine Chappell, out of long personal experience, has voiced the ideal such setting apart holds before all servants of God:

"For their sakes, I sanctify myself;"
For these people's sakes, O my Lord;
These people amongst whom I move, the unfriendly,
The indifferent, the unkind, the antagonistic—
For their sakes, O Beloved Master, I separate
Myself in Thy name; from my will to Thy will,
From my way to Thy way;

I lay at Thy feet, for their sakes, all carelessness
About my spirit, my words, my tone, my manner.
I desire to serve them to the full, not only
In my office but in my life, myself, my all;
And therefore, that I may get at them, I come
To Thee. That I may win them
I separate myself unto Thee.

Sixth, the ministry is *a challenge.* It is the greatest task ever committed to human hands. There is nothing higher, harder, or holier among men than to minister the unsearchable riches of Christ. No occupation is more elevating, more exacting, more exalted. It would be a step down to become president of the United States or prime minister of Great Britain. Samuel Chadwick is quoted as having said, "I would rather preach than eat my dinner or have a holiday. I would rather pay to preach than be paid not to preach. It has its place in the agony of sweat and tears. No calling has such joys and heartbreak, but it is a calling an archangel might covet and I thank God that in His grace He called me into His ministry."[32]

The ministry is the only profession among men with eternal consequences. Christ told Peter and his fellow apostles that, in their work of making known what had been bound or loosed in heaven, they would actually be in possession of "the keys of the kingdom" (Matt. 16:19). All other professions have value for earth and for time alone. The ministry of the gospel has value for earth and for time, but beyond that for heaven and for eternity as well. The doctor of medicine may relieve pain and extend the span of mortal life, but in the end he loses every patient he treats. He finally turns them over to the undertaker, unless he himself goes first. On the other hand, when through the healing power of divine grace wholeness comes to a sin-diseased soul, a work has been done that will have consequences when the sun has grown cold and the stars have lost their fire. Beyond measure, indeed, is the challenge of the ministry.

Finally, the ministry is a *continuation* of Christ's ministry on earth. "I have chosen you, and ordained you," Jesus said, "that ye should go and bring forth fruit, and that your fruit should remain" (John 15:16). "As my Father hath sent me, even so send I you" (John 20:21).

The whole Church, and especially its ministry, is the continuing ministry of Christ in this world. He speaks when His Word is proclaimed. He helps and heals when hands of mercy are extended to those in

[32]Mimeographed bulletin, no source given.

need. Even opposition to His followers is opposition to Him, for Saul of Tarsus was reined up short on the Damascus road with the question, "Why persecutest thou me?" As Geoffrey Bromiley expressed it, Christ exercises "a continuing ministry of word and sacrament, action and passion, through the ministers whom He has chosen, ordained, commissioned and sent out as His witnesses in the world. The ministry of the apostles, indeed of all Christian ministers, of all Christians and the whole Christian community, is in the first and last resort the continuing ministry of Jesus."[33]

The human figure is the instrument; Christ himself is the true Minister. It is, Paul said, "as though God did beseech you by us: we pray you in Christ's stead, be ye reconciled to God" (II Cor. 5:20). It is the thought Margaret Clarkson has captured in her beautiful lines:

So send I you to bind the bruised and broken;
O'er wand'ring souls to work, to weep, to wake;
To bear the burdens of a world aweary.
So send I you to suffer for My sake.

So send I you to leave your life's ambition,
To die to dear desire, self-will resign;
To labor long and love where men revile you.
So send I you to lose your life in Mine.

So send I you to hearts made hard by hatred,
To eyes made blind because they will not see;
To spend, though it be blood—to spend and spare not.
So send I you to taste of Calvary.[34]

[33]*Christian Ministry* (Grand Rapids, Mich.: Wm. B. Eerdmans Publishing Co., 1959), p. 16.

[34]Copyright, Zondervan Publishing House. Used by permission.

CHAPTER 2

An Outline of the Biblical Image

The next four chapters of this study will be devoted to four major elements in the New Testament image of the minister. In this chapter, we shall be concerned with some of the more limited terms used to describe the pastor's character and work. These are, so to speak, the lighter lines in the picture, the detail and shading in the portrait. We are almost embarrassed by the amazing wealth of imagery, the richness of detail and description employed to describe the work of the ministry.

I

Behind the New Testament image of the ministry is the Old Testament picture describing the functions of priest, prophet, and wise man.

The Levitical order with its appointed service of Tabernacle and Temple and its Aaronic priesthood is the earliest indication of a specially designated ministry. The priesthood was the great conservator of institutional religion among the covenant people of God. As such, it represents an aspect of the spiritual life that is essential.

To the priests of the Old Testament was entrusted the Torah, that is, the Law, the instruction and guidance of the people in everyday life. The priests served as mediators between God and man. They offered the sacrifices in behalf of the people. They conveyed the blessing of the Lord upon the congregation in the unforgettable lines of the Levitical benediction: "The Lord bless thee, and keep thee: the Lord make his face shine upon thee, and be gracious unto thee: the Lord lift up his countenance upon thee, and give thee peace" (Num. 6:24-26). They were, in a real sense, the pastors of the people.

But the priesthood had all the built-in liabilities of any hereditary order. It was subject to corruption. It lacked capacity for self-renewal. Its function had to be supplemented by the prophet, as both seer (*ro'eh*) and speaker (*nabi*). As has often been said, the prophet in Scripture is less the foreteller and more the forthteller of the will of God—recognizing, of course, that forthtelling often included foretelling.

Th. C. Vriezen claims that "the prophet is the typical and the most important figure in the Old Testament."[1] "The prophet is the man who speaks, who carries the Word of God," he goes on.[2] The prophets were men "who knew the intimacy of fellowship with God, to whom something of his spirit was given, men who looked on the world in the light of what they had seen in the heart of God, men who spoke because they had to and not because they wanted to, upon whom the

[1] *An Outline of Old Testament Theology* (Boston: Charles T. Branford Company, 1958), p. 256.

[2] *Ibid.*, p. 258.

constraint of God had been laid, and men who delivered a word not alone relevant to the needs of the hour, but of enduring importance to men."[3]

It has often been assumed that the prophets were antagonistic toward Temple and priesthood and that their criticisms of ritual and sacrifice were directed at the institutions themselves. Further reflection has put this in clearer light. Not only are there conspicuous examples of prophets who were themselves priests (as, for instance, Jeremiah and Ezekiel), but it is increasingly clear that the objections of the prophets were directed, not against ritual itself, but against empty ritual; not just against sacrifice, but against sacrifice without loyalty and love.

There are, to be sure, some temperamental types that incline toward what is more central in the priestly order, and some that lean more toward what is seen in the "charismatic existence" of the prophet.[4] Kyle Yates describes the tensions that may exist between these two types of personality in these words:

> In the religious history of the world two types of mind invariably collide: the priestly and the prophetic. The priest puts the prime emphasis on worship and finds joy in ceremonies and ritual observances. He is apt to be a conservative who finds it difficult to worship God except by means of elaborate ceremonies and liturgies. Morality has a place in his theology but it is not a prime place. Formalism becomes one of his biggest sins for religion tends to become mere form. The prophet lays the chief emphasis on life, on conduct, on moral quality. He is constantly opposing the person who depends on mere perfunctory performance

[3]H. H. Rowley, *The Faith of Israel: Aspects of Old Testament Thought* (Philadelphia: The Westminster Press, 1956), p. 39.

[4]Cf. Ludwig Kohler, *Old Testament Theology,* trans. A. S. Todd (Philadelphia: The Westminster Press, 1957), p. 165.

of regular duties. He irritates, prods, denounces, stands alone in his demands, insists on applying God's eternal principles to life. To him conduct is much more important than ceremonies. He is an ethical teacher, a moral reformer, a dangerous disturber of men's minds. He constantly strikes at sins, vices and lapses and seeks to stir men to holier lives.[5]

Actually, of course, both institutional and charismatic elements are essential.[6] D. R. Davies in *On to Orthodoxy* makes the point that the minister of today must combine within himself the functions of priest and prophet. He says:

> The contradiction of the ministry is that ministers have to be both prophets and priests. They have to be both revolutionaries and statesmen. And that is very difficult. In caring for the Church as an organization, the minister is a priest or statesman. In his concern for the Church as a vehicle of God's Spirit in History, he is a prophet. Only too often the priest suppresses the prophet. Much more rarely, the prophet abolishes the priest. Unless the minister is a prophet, there is a danger of a famine of "the word of the Lord." Unless he is also a priest, there is peril that the institution may disintegrate. The only solution is to preserve the tension and for the minister to be both.[7]

Walther Eichrodt describes the creativity of this tension as it appears in the Old Testament and carries over into the New:

> The religion of the Old Testament only unfolded the richness of its tensions through the interplay of prophecy and priesthood; and this richness was both exalted into a higher unity in the primitive Christian gospel, and also emerged in new forms as a result of its ap-

[5]*Preaching from the Prophets* (New York: Harper and Brothers, 1942), p. 7.

[6]Cf. Vriezen, *op. cit.*, p. 266.

[7](New York: The Macmillan Co., 1949), p. 197.

> propriation by Christianity. Ultimately it is the tension between the God who has come and the God who is to come, between the revealed and the hidden God, between the God who has entered into earthly corporality and the God throned in eternal majesty, which, though beyond the scope of human conception, is yet made vividly clear in Christ; and this ambivalence of God's manifestation in the world both keeps human reflection in perpetual turmoil, and yet, when affirmed in faith and obedience, leads men to the divine fullness of the biblical revelation.[8]

Yet when we pass into the New Testament, it is the prophetic emphasis that comes to the fore. As Yates points out with respect to Jesus,

> His emphasis was the prophetic emphasis. Men must change their lives, behave as godly creatures, put the emphasis where the prophet has always put it. He did not once call Himself a priest. When His disciples were asked to give their estimate of Him they called the names of several prophets but not a single priest. The author of Hebrews speaks of Him as a priest but quickly warns against the thought that he has any connection with the priestly group since the day of Melchizedek. When Christianity lost its power and became a priestly religion the emphasis was naturally shifted from conduct to ceremonies. The natural result came about and the church with gorgeous ritual and elaborate ceremonies became immoral and failed in its prophetic mission. This will ever be true when we fail to show concern for vital religion that issues in godly conduct.[9]

The prophet in the Old Testament was often known as the *man of God,* a phrase also used in the New Testament. Moses was so designated in Deut. 33:1 and Josh. 14:6, as were the unnamed prophet of I Sam.

[8]*Theology of the Old Testament,* trans. J. A. Baker (Philadelphia: The Westminster Press, 1961), I, 436.

[9]*Op. cit.,* p. 7.

2:27, Samuel (I Sam. 9:6), Shemaiah (I Kings 12:22), Elijah (I Kings 17:18, 24), and others. The phrase was also used as a title synonymous with *prophet* in the sense of the true prophet of the Lord as contrasted with the many false prophets of Old Testament times (I Kings 13:1, 6-8, 12; 17:24; 20:28; II Kings 1:9; etc.).

The prophet was also known as a *watchman.* Isaiah speaks of the voice calling to him out of Seir and addressing him with the words, "Watchman, what of the night? Watchman, what of the night?" (Isa. 21:11) The curse of any people is to have blind watchmen, dumb dogs that cannot bark, shepherds that cannot understand (Isa. 56:10-11). Jeremiah tells of the watchmen God had set over the people, to warn them with the sound of the trumpet (Jer. 6:17), and Ezekiel is appointed a watchman unto the house of Israel charged with life-and-death responsibility to warn of approaching danger (Ezek. 3:17-21; 33:2-6). Hosea (9:8) and Micah (7:4) use the same comparison.

Again, the prophet in the Old Testament is known as the *servant of the Lord.* Moses is commonly so titled (Exod. 14:31; Josh. 9:24; I Chron. 6:49; II Chron. 24:9; Neh. 10:29); as were Joshua (Josh. 5:14) and Daniel (Dan. 6:20). Commenting on Paul's use of the term servant in relation to his own office as apostle, William Barclay writes, "But this word slave (*doulos*) has another side to it. In the Old Testament it is the regular word which describes the great men of God. Moses was the servant, the slave, the *doulos* of the Lord (Joshua 1:2). Joshua himself was the *doulos* of God (Joshua 24:9). The proudest title of the prophets, the title which distinguishes them from other men, is that they are the servants and the slaves of God (Amos 3:7; Jeremiah 7:25). When Paul calls himself the slave of Jesus Christ he is doing nothing less than setting himself in the succession of the prophets."[10]

II

Turning to the New Testament, we find imagery of two major kinds describing the ministry. There is, first, a series of images in the quite literal sense of metaphor, comparison, or analogy. There is, second, a list of terms whose generic meanings contribute to the image of the ministry in the broader sense of concept, the controlling idea or coloring thought descriptive of the preacher's task.

1. In the first category, the earliest term applied to a preacher is *messenger,* literally *angelos* (Mark 1:2), the same Greek term translated "angel" in Revelation 2 and 3 in connection with the seven churches of Asia Minor. With due respect for the exegesis which would see in the "angels" of the seven churches heavenly guardians or representatives, it scarcely seems likely that Christ would give His servant John on earth messages to heavenly beings ordinarily beyond the ken of mortal men. As a messenger, the minister comes with a gospel which he did not originate and whose terms he does not dictate. And he comes with the authority and weight of Him who sends the message.

2. The term *messenger* is used of John the Baptist, who is also spoken of as *the voice of one crying in the wilderness,* a quotation from Isa. 40:3 found in all four Gospels (Mark 1:3; Matt. 3:3; Luke 3:4; John 1:23). E. Stanley Jones recalls the entry in the minutes of an old New England church: "A committee was appointed to examine the squeak in the pulpit." Dr. Jones com-

[10]*The Letter to the Romans* (Philadelphia: The Westminster Press, 1957), p. 2.

ments: "There are a lot of ministers who could answer that description—'a squeak in the pulpit.' The real man of God is not a 'squeak,' but a Voice. He sounds out eternal verities in a positive way and produces positive results."[11]

3. *Fishermen,* or "fishers of men," is another designation of the ministry in the Gospels (Mark 1:17-18; Matt. 4:19; Luke 5:10). Akira Hatori at the World Congress on Evangelism in Berlin said a fisherman friend gave him three secrets of successful fishing: go where the fish are; choose a good time; use skill.[12] Certainly skill and persistence are qualities of a successful fisherman. To this might be added the ability to choose bait that appeals to the fish. It is interesting to listen to fishermen talk about their variety of lures. What has worked one time may not work another time. The smart fisherman changes his lures until he finds those the fish are taking.

4. *Shepherd* is an Old Testament designation brought over into gospel terminology by Jesus in the saying recorded in John 10:12 in which shepherds and hirelings are contrasted: "He that is an hireling, and not the shepherd, whose own the sheep are not, seeth the wolf coming, and leaveth the sheep, and fleeth: and the wolf catcheth them, and scattereth the sheep." While there is a valid exegetical question as to whether the shepherd here refers to any other than "the good shepherd" of vv. 11 and 14, the use of the same term for human ministers by Paul in Eph. 4:11 ("pastors") gives some measure of sanction to the well-entrenched

[11]*Growing Spiritually* (Nashville: Abingdon Press, 1953), p. 108.

[12]November 3, 1966, Berlin, West Germany.

extension of "shepherd" to the under-shepherds of Christ's diffused flock.

5. A term introduced in the Gospels (Luke 24:48) and prominent throughout the Acts of the Apostles is the striking word *witness*. The "Golden Text" of Acts employs it: "But ye shall receive power, after that the Holy Ghost is come upon you: and ye shall be witnesses unto me both in Jerusalem, and in all Judaea, and in Samaria, and unto the uttermost part of the earth" (1:8). The apostolic company accepted it: one must be ordained in place of Judas "to be a witness with us of his resurrection" (1:22; cf. 2:32; 3:15; 5:32; etc.). Paul was made "a minister and a witness" (26:16).

This point could well justify a chapter in itself. Bishop William Quayle said, "Preaching is the art of making a sermon and delivering it. Why no, that is not preaching. Preaching is the art of making a preacher, and delivering that. Preaching is the outrush of soul in speech. Therefore the elemental business in preaching is not with the preaching but with the preacher. It is no trouble to preach, but a vast trouble to construct a preacher. What, then, in the light of this is the task of the preacher? Mainly this, the amassing of a great soul so as to have something worth while to give—the sermon is the preacher up to date."[13] President Woodrow Wilson used to quote his father, a Presbyterian minister, as saying, "The Christian minister must *be* something before he can *do* anything."[14]

6. The Acts of the Apostles introduces two additional terms for the minister. The first of these is *vessel*

[13]Quoted, William Barclay, *Fishers of Men* (Philadelphia: The Westminster Press, 1966), p. 37.

[14]Quoted, John C. Thiessen, *Pastoring the Smaller Church* (Grand Rapids, Mich.: Zondervan Publishing House, 1962), p. 39.

(9:15). Saul of Tarsus was introduced to the fearful Ananias as "a chosen vessel unto me, to bear my name before the Gentiles, and kings, and the children of Israel." The great apostle himself later referred to the treasure of the gospel as being deposited in "earthen vessels." One enterprising seminarian, referring to the fact that no doubt some of the vessels are chipped and cracked, announced as the title of a sermon on this text, "The Glory of the Cracked Pot."

7. The second term used in the Acts is *servant* (*doulos,* 16:17). The word literally means slave. As we have seen, it was used of the prophets of the Old Testament. It is introduced as a designation for the minister in the New Testament under the dubious circumstance of being voiced by the girl with the spirit of divination who cried out that Paul and others of his company were "the servants of the most high God." Paul used it of himself as a title in the opening verses of his letters to Rome and Philippi, and to Titus (Rom. 1:1; Phil. 1:1; Titus 1:1); as also did James (1:1), Peter (II Pet. 1:1), Jude (1), and John (Rev. 1:1). It is, as Archibald Hunter notes, the perfect correlate for "Lord" and implies the most complete and total subjection to the will and purposes of the Master. The servant of New Testament times was most typically a slave. He was the property of another. His total life was subject to the will of the man he called "Lord." There were, it may be said, no part-time slaves and no slaves who punched time clocks. Every minute of every day belonged to the master. Life for the slave was what his owner willed it to be.

Paul's Corinthian correspondence, or that portion of it preserved for us in the New Testament, contributes five additional descriptive terms in this category of metaphors of the ministry. This is as we might expect, recalling the background of challenge to his apostolic office against which the apostle wrote.

8. In I Cor. 3:9, Paul speaks of himself and other ministers as *fellow laborers*. "We are labourers together with God: ye are God's husbandry [tilled land], ye are God's building." The participle form is used in the Greek of II Cor. 6:1, "We then, as workers together with him, beseech you that ye receive not the grace of God in vain."

The term here, *sunergos,* is variously translated "fellow labourer," "fellow worker," "companion in labour," or "fellow helper" (III John 8). It represents not so much the toil of the task as the necessity for teamwork. No shepherd of Christ's flock can be a "lone wolf." To the extent the *prima donna* seems to succeed, it is as a parasite feeding on the unacknowledged toil of others.

9. In this same context, in the following verse, one kind of labor is mentioned. The apostle speaks of himself as a *masterbuilder,* an *architeckton,* laying the foundation upon which others would build. The idea here, as Paul Deitenbeck has suggested, is that of an assistant architect.[15] He is a "working foreman," able to plan tasks for himself and for others. His is no desk in an air-conditioned architect's office, as the papyri and inscriptions plainly show. He is at home on the job. While he sees farther than the common laborers with whom he works, he does not shun their toil and strain.

10. In I Cor. 4:1-2, Paul describes the ministers of Christ as "*stewards* of the mysteries of God," the indispensable requirement of whom is not brilliance or outstanding achievement but faithfulness. The *oikono-*

[15]At the World Congress on Evangelism, Berlin, November 3, 1966.

mos was literally the "house arranger." He was the manager of the household or estate. He had, as we learn from Luke 16:1-12, a wide range of discretion in the handling of his master's affairs. Yet he was strictly accountable for his administration of the affairs committed to his care.

11. The minister is also like an *athlete,* specifically a runner or a boxer. "Know ye not that they which run in a race run all, but one receiveth the prize? So run, that ye may obtain. And every man that striveth for the mastery is temperate in all things. Now they do it to obtain a corruptible crown; but we an incorruptible. I therefore so run, not as uncertainly; so fight I, not as one that beateth the air: but I keep under my body, and bring it into subjection: lest that by any means, when I have preached to others, I myself should be a castaway" (I Cor. 9:24-27).

The same figure is used in II Tim. 2:5, "And if a man strive for masteries, yet is he not crowned, except he strive lawfully." The phrase here translated "strive for masteries" comes from a single word, *athleo,* and means striving in games, or wrestling. The crown in question was the wreath of triumph given the victor. The implication is obvious. Discipline, training, single-minded dedication, and "playing by the rules" are the qualities of the winning athlete. Do we do less who seek for a crown that fades not away (I Pet. 5:4) as the garlands of oak, ivy, myrtle, or olive would fade on the brow of a Greek decathlon victor?

12. In II Cor. 5:20, Paul uses the term "*ambassadors* for Christ" to describe the function of those who beseech men "in Christ's stead" to be "reconciled to God." In Eph. 6:19, the apostle speaks of himself as "an ambassador in bonds." The idea behind the word is that of authority and dignity.

William Barclay gives an unforgettable example of the nature of the ambassadorial mission in his Daily Bible Study on *The Epistle to the Hebrews*:

> On one occasion the king of Syria, Antiochus Epiphanes, invaded Egypt. Rome desired to stop him. Rome sent an envoy called Popillius to tell Antiochus to abandon his projected invasion. Popillius caught up with him on the borders of Egypt. Antiochus and Popillius talked of this and that for they had known each other in Rome. Popillius had not the vestige of an army with him, not even a guard, no force at all. Finally Antiochus asked him why he had come. Quietly Popillius told him that he had come to tell him that Rome wished him to abandon the invasion and go home. "I will consider it," said Antiochus. Popillius smiled a little grimly; he took his staff and drew a circle in the earth around Antiochus. "Consider it," he said, "and come to your decision before you leave that circle." Antiochus thought for a few seconds and then he said: "Very well, then. I will go home." Popillius himself had not the slightest force available—but behind him was all the authority of the empire from which he came.[16]

13. From Eph. 4:11-12 comes the suggestion out of which Elton Trueblood has drawn the idea of the minister as a *"playing coach."*[17] Apostles, prophets, evangelists, pastors, and teachers are given for "the equipping of the saints to the work of ministry" (lit.). The total alteration of the sense of this passage by the insertion of a comma after "saints" in the King James Version has often been noted. It is the perfecting of the saints for the work of ministering that is the task of apostles, prophets, evangelists, pastors, and teachers. It is the ministry of the laity that is here in view, and the

[16] (Philadelphia: The Westminster Press, 1955), p. 24.

[17] Trueblood, *op. cit.*, p. 43.

ministerial offices named are held, as T. W. Manson said, by those who are "just laymen who have lost their amateur status."[18]

14. A somewhat limited designation is found in Philemon 1, where Paul calls himself *a prisoner of Jesus Christ.* That there is a reference here to his Roman incarceration is scarcely to be denied. But it is significant that the apostle refuses to give Nero and the Romans credit for his imprisonment, and identifies himself as the prisoner of Jesus Christ. Paul used another form of the same Greek term when he spoke of going "bound in the spirit unto Jerusalem" (Acts 20:22), constrained by inner bonds that held him to a course others advised against.

15. The letters to Timothy add three more metaphors to our already lengthy list. The minister is a *pattern* (*hupotuposis,* I Tim. 1:16; *tupos,* Titus 2:7) and an *example.* "Howbeit for this cause I obtained mercy, that in me first Jesus Christ might shew forth all longsuffering, for a pattern to them which should hereafter believe on him to life everlasting" (I Tim. 1:16). "In all things shewing thyself a pattern of good works" (Titus 2:7).

There is a note here we must never lose. The minister must honestly be able to say, "Follow me as I follow Christ." He must exemplify in himself what he essays to preach. As William Temple put it, "It is quite futile saying to people: 'Go to the cross.' We must be able to say: 'Come to the Cross.' And there are only two voices which can issue that invitation with effect. One is the voice of the sinless Redeemer, with which we cannot speak; and one is the voice of the

[18]Quoted by Anthony T. Hanson, *The Church of the Servant* (Naperville, Ill.: SCM Book Club, 1962), p. 61.

forgiven sinner, who knows himself forgiven. That is our part."[19]

16. The minister is a *soldier,* "a good soldier of Jesus Christ" (II Tim. 2:3). Therefore he must keep himself disentangled from the affairs of this life (v. 4). To entangle is literally "to weave into," become part of the warp and woof of. What this injunction may mean to the individual preacher of the gospel must be conscientiously faced within the context of his own life. Needless to say, failure to take it seriously can result in failure to be a good soldier of Jesus Christ.

17. The minister is explicitly called a ***husbandman*** in II Tim. 2:6, "The husbandman that laboureth must be first partaker of the fruits." The groundwork for this metaphor was laid in I Cor. 3:6-8, "I have planted, Apollos watered; but God gave the increase. So then neither is he that planteth any thing, neither he that watereth; but God that giveth the increase. Now he that planteth and he that watereth are one: and every man shall receive his own reward according to his own labour."

The husbandman is the tiller of the ground, the vinedresser, or as we would say, the farmer. He labors not only in consciousness of his need of others, but also in consciousness of his dependence upon God. He is, as Jesus had said, "a sower" who goes forth to sow seed fully aware that some will fall on hard and trampled ground, other on the thinly covered rock, other among thorns and briars. Yet he sows because some falls into good ground and brings forth fruit unto salvation, some 30, some 60, and some 100 fold.

[19]*Towards the Conversion of England,* p. 66; quoted by Leighton Ford, *The Christian Persuader* (New York: Harper and Row, 1966), p. 138.

III

We turn from this varied and impressive list of images in the quite literal sense of metaphor to a group of terms with more generic meaning. These relate to image in the broader sense of concept or controlling idea, what comes to mind when the subject is mentioned. Admittedly, there is a very fine line between some of the terms in this series and the kind of terms explored as metaphors—particularly when we go behind the connotations of the more familiar English to their Greek originals. There is, of course, a metaphorical element in all language. Yet the distinction seems to be sufficient to justify some attempt at a classification such as this.

1. *Disciple* is the first of these terms. Because special attention will be given to this in the next chapter, it will be merely mentioned here. It is the broad term for all Christians—"The disciples were called Christians first in Antioch" (Acts 11:26)—and means both learner and one who follows the teachings of another. The disciple is not only a pupil. He is also an adherent. Before the earliest Christian ministers were apostles, they were disciples (Matt. 5:1; 10:1; Luke 22:11).

2. *Apostle* is for our purpose the more significant term common to the whole New Testament literature to designate those specially chosen and sent. It was Jesus' own title for the 12 He selected. "And when it was day, he called unto him his disciples: and of them he chose twelve, whom also he named apostles" (Luke 6:13)—and the emphatic "also" in the Greek implies that the apostles are still disciples. The term "apostle" comes from *apo,* "from," and *stello,* "to send." It is therefore literally "one sent forth."

It is important to note that the New Testament

uses *apostle* in both a narrow and technical sense as designating the original Twelve, and in a broad and etymological sense describing those specially authorized messengers or representatives sent forth by the Church. In the narrow sense, the apostolate is the group of men who had been companions of Jesus during His public ministry and who were officially designated as witnesses to His resurrection (Acts 1:22). Paul was added to this company by a unique sort of divine action in the appearance of Christ to him on the Damascus road. It was through the apostolate that the New Testament scriptures were given, pre-validated by Jesus himself (Luke 10:16; John 17:20). As witnesses to the Resurrection in the strictest sense, the apostolic company was necessarily limited to that one generation.

Yet the New Testament also uses the term apostle in the broader and nontechnical sense already alluded to. Barnabas (Acts 14:4, 14), Andronicus and Junius (Rom. 16:7), Epaphroditus ("your apostle," Phil. 2:25, probably in the sense of one specially sent and authorized to act as agent by the Philippian church), and Silas and Timothy (I Thess. 2:6) are identified by name as apostles. It is probable also that Paul, in Eph. 4:11, thought of both apostles and prophets as continuing offices in the Church. As is true of other of these generic terms for the ministry, the word apostle implies an authorized and authoritative representation of God to men by men.

3. *Elder,* in the sense of a position of responsibility in the Christian community, occurs first in the Acts of the Apostles: "Then the disciples, every man according to his ability, determined to send relief unto the brethren which dwelt in Judaea: which also they did, and sent it to the elders by the hands of Barnabas and Saul" (Acts 11:29-30). While there is not in the New Testa-

ment the formal meaning attached to the term in our present usage, there is evidence of selection for and ordination to the eldership (Acts 14:23; I Tim. 5:17, 19; Titus 1:5). The broad function of those termed elders is described by the verb *episkopeo* (Acts 20:17, 28; Titus 1:5, 7), overseeing, serving as bishops. The elders (*presbyteroi*) were charged with the spiritual care and oversight of the churches.

4. *Bishop* or *overseer* is a term equated with elder in Acts 20:17, 28. The elders of the church at Ephesus had been made overseers (*episkopoi*) or bishops of the flock and were charged to "feed the church of God, which he hath purchased with his own blood." The term in the original comes from *epi,* "over," and *skopeo,* "to look or watch." Besides its use in Acts, the term is found in relation to an office in the church in Phil. 1:1; I Tim. 3:2; and Titus 1:7. In I Pet. 2:25, Christ is spoken of as "the Shepherd and Bishop of your souls." The related *episkope* is translated "bishoprick" in Acts 1:20, and the verb *episkopeo* occurs in some texts of I Pet. 5:2, where it is translated "taking the oversight thereof": "The elders which are among you I exhort . . . feed the flock of God which is among you, taking the oversight thereof, not by constraint, but willingly" (I Pet. 5:1-2). There are in the term, therefore, both administrative and pastoral overtones. I Thess. 5:12-13 would seem to identify the work of elders and overseers as that which we would call typically the pastoral ministry.

5. *Minister* is the single English word used to translate three Greek terms, each with somewhat different background and meaning. First, there is the minister as *huperetes,* literally an under rower in distinction from a seaman. It therefore came to apply to anyone who serves as an assistant acting under another's orders. It

was the term applied to John Mark, who was the "minister" to Barnabas and Saul (Acts 13:5); and to Paul himself when Christ designated him to be "a minister and a witness" both of the things he had seen and of that in which the Lord would yet appear unto him (Acts 26:16). It is applied to Apollos and Peter in I Cor. 4:1. Something of its meaning is seen in its use in Luke 4:20 to describe the attendant of the scrolls in the synagogue and its frequent use to designate the officers, attendants, or bailiffs of magistrates, synagogues, or the Sanhedrin (e.g., Matt. 5:25; 26:58; Mark 14:54, 65; John 7:32, 45-46; 18:3, 12, 18, 22; 19:6; Acts 5:22, 26).

Second, there is the minister as *diakonos,* the source of our familiar word deacon and primarily meaning servant, whatever the nature of the service. It is probably derived from *dioko,* "following after or pursuing." It is applied to domestics (John 2:5, 9), to civil rulers (Rom. 13:4), Christ himself (Rom. 15:8; Gal. 2:17), and many times of the followers of Christ apart from any specified ministerial function (e.g., Matt. 20:26; 23:11; Mark 9:35; 10:43; John 12:27; Rom. 16:1; Eph. 6:21; Col. 1:7; 4:7). It is used in connection with preaching and teaching in I Cor. 3:5; II Cor. 3:6; 6:4; 11:23; Eph. 3:7; Col. 1:23, 25; I Thess. 3:2; and I Tim. 4:6. It is even used of emissaries of Satan who are described as "his ministers" and are "transformed as the minsters of righteousness" (II Cor. 11:15).

Third, there is the minister as *leitourgos,* from which we derive the term liturgy. It means, principally, one who discharges public office. It is used but twice in the New Testament as related to a function in the Church. Paul speaks of himself as "the minister of Jesus Christ to the Gentiles, ministering the gospel of God, that the offering up of the Gentiles might be acceptable, being sanctified by the Holy Ghost" (Rom. 15:16). Epaphroditus, already introduced as the messenger (apostle) of the Philippians to Paul, is also said to have ministered to the apostle's wants (Phil. 2:25). It may be admitted that both of these usages are in an adapted sense. Christ (Heb. 8:2), angels (Heb. 1:7), and earthly magistrates (Rom. 13:6) are also described as ministers in the sense of *leitourgoi.*

6. *Preacher,* a herald or one who makes a proclamation, occurs in Rom. 10:14; I Tim. 2:7; II Tim. 1:11; and II Pet. 2:5. Since major consideration is to be given to this later, it will be merely noted here that the relatively rare use of the noun (or participle, in Rom. 10:14) is more than balanced by the strong and constant use of the verbs denoting the action of preaching.

7. *Prophet,* from *pro,* "forth," and *phemi,* "to speak," is more closely related to preacher than we have usually been aware. The New Testament uses the term in several distinct senses: in relation to the Old Testament prophets (Matt. 5:12; Mark 6:15; Luke 4:27; Rom. 11:3; etc.); of prophets in general (Matt. 10:41; 21:46); of John the Baptist (Matt. 21:26; Luke 1:76); of Jesus both as *the* Prophet (John 1:21; 6:14; Acts 3:22; 7:37) and as *a* Prophet (Mark 6:15; Luke 7:16; John 4:19; etc.).

Of special interest to us in this context are the references to prophets in the churches, of which there are several (e.g., Acts 13:1; 15:32; 21:10; I Cor. 12:28-29; 14:29, 32, 37; Eph. 2:20; 3:5; 4:11), as well as references to the gift of prophecy (Rom. 12:6; I Cor. 12:10; 14:5). The function of prophecy in the New Testament sense is clearly outlined in I Cor. 14:3, "But he that prophesieth speaketh unto men to edification, and exhortation, and comfort."

It should be noted that, both by derivation and by

relation to its Old Testament background, prophecy is much more than predicting or foretelling the future. It is "the speaking forth of the mind and counsel of God."[20] "It is the declaration of that which cannot be known by natural means, Matt. 26:68, it is the forth-telling of the will of God, whether with reference to the past, the present, or the future."[21]

It has been contended from I Cor. 13:8-9 that the gifts of prophecy and tongues passed out of the Church on the completion of the New Testament canon. While not being contentious at the point of the exegesis here, one may well point out that to the extent the preacher of today speaks to men to edification, exhortation, and comfort, to that degree he exercises the prophetic office and to that degree he manifests the prophetic gift.

In addition to two already treated, a cluster of three other great terms is found in Eph. 4:11, "And he gave some, apostles; and some, prophets; and some, evangelists; and some, pastors and teachers."

8. The *evangelist* is literally the messenger of good. He is not the one who brings the gossip, as the little girl said; but the one who brings the gospel, the good news of salvation. Philip was designated "the evangelist" (Acts 21:8), and Timothy is exhorted to "do the work of an evangelist, make full proof of thy ministry" (II Tim. 4:5). As with the term preacher, the frequency of the action form, "to proclaim glad tidings," makes up for the comparative rarity of the noun.

9. As in the English, so in the Greek, there is a close connection almost amounting to identification be-

[20]W. E. Vine, *An Expository Dictionary of New Testament Words* (London: Oliphants, Ltd., 1940), III, 221.

[21]*Ibid.*, quoted from *Notes on Thessalonians* by Hogg and Vine, p. 196.

tween *"pastors* and *teachers."* We have noted briefly the derivation of pastor from *shepherd,* and will return to the pastoral function for major consideration later. *Teacher* (*didaskalos*) is used in a normative sense for a function in the Church in Acts 13:1; I Cor. 12:28-29; I Tim. 2:7; II Tim. 1:11; Heb. 5:12; and Jas. 3:1. It is frequently used of Christ in the Gospels, where it is often translated "Master" or "Rabbi."

A caution certainly ought to be inserted at this point against too easy acceptance of the modern distinction between preaching and teaching, growing out of the sharp separation of "kerygma" and "didache," made by some New Testament scholars. That there is a distinction may be recognized. Yet the fact is that all Christian preaching involves teaching; and all teaching, if it is Christian, includes proclamation. One or the other may be preeminent, but both must be present if the message and meaning of the gospel are to be communicated.

10. Twice in the New Testament the minister is titled *the man of God.* "But thou, O man of God, flee these things; and follow after righteousness, godliness, faith, love, patience, meekness" (I Tim. 6:11). The function of Scripture is "that the man of God may be perfect, throughly furnished unto all good works" (II Tim. 3:17).

11. Only in a secondary sense is the minister ever referred to as a *priest* in the New Testament, and then in connection with the familiar Protestant affirmation of the priesthood of all believers. In I Pet. 2:9, we are part of "a royal priesthood," a thought paralleled in Rev. 1:6, where God is said to have "made us kings and priests." Yet in a particular way the minister may serve as the representative of his people with God, that is, as their priest, when he intercedes for them either in public or in private. As William Barclay has pointed

out, the Latin for priest is *pontifex,* literally "bridge builder," and the minister must build bridges between God and man.[22]

Peter Forsyth reminds us that the priestly function of the minister in prayer may have a cathartic effect upon the man's own spirit. "The *intercessory* private prayer of the minister is the best corrective of the *critical* spirit or the grumbling spirit which so easily besets and withers us to-day. That reconciliation, that pacification of heart, which comes by prayer opens in us a fountain of private intercession, especially for our antagonists." He adds, "Only, of course, it must be private."[23]

We have come to the end of a long and somewhat meandering journey, tracing the lines—minor and major—in the biblical image of the minister. "Who," we may ask with another, "is sufficient for these things?" The communicator of the Word partakes of the nature of priest, prophet, wise man, and watchman. He is a messenger, a voice, a fisherman, a shepherd. He is a vessel, a servant, a laborer, a master builder, a steward. He is athlete, ambassador, pattern, soldier, and husbandman. He is disciple, apostle, elder, overseer, minister, preacher, herald, evangelist, pastor, and teacher. Above all, he is a man of God, and in spirit and morale should stand no less than 10 feet tall.

[22]*Fishers of Men,* p. 65.

[23]*The Soul of Prayer* (Grand Rapids: Wm. B. Eerdmans Publishing Co., 1916), p. 77.

CHAPTER 3

The Minister as Student

In Paul's last letter, there is a revealing personal note that gives a wealth of insight into the great apostle's concept of his calling. He was writing to Timothy about coming to him in Rome, urging him to come before winter. He counselled the younger man to "preach the word"; to "be instant in season, out of season"; to "reprove, rebuke, exhort with all longsuffering and doctrine." He warned against a coming impatience with sound theology, and spoke of a time when people with itching ears would seek teachers who would tell them what they wanted to hear. He urged Timothy to do the work of an evangelist and to make full proof of his ministry.

For himself, Paul said, he was ready to be offered. The time of his departure was at hand. He had fought a good fight. He had finished the course. He had kept the faith. He was confident of a crown of righteousness which the Lord, the righteous Judge, would give him. Demas had forsaken him, having loved the present world. Others had been sent on errands in the gospel work.

Only Luke was with him. Timothy was instructed to bring Mark when he came, for the young man who had once failed had since proved himself and was profitable in the ministry.

Then comes a note purely personal. Timothy was instructed to bring the cloak that had been left at Troas with Carpus—"and the books, but especially the parchments" (II Tim. 4:13). Right down to the very end of his life, Paul was a student desiring his books and parchments, the latter probably being copies of the Old Testament scriptures.

I

No minister ever outgrows the need for the disciplines of the study. College commencement may give him an A.B., the first two letters of the alphabet. Seminary or graduate work may have added two or three more. But the rest of the alphabet is strictly up to him in a program of lifelong learning.

Failure to cultivate the books and especially the parchments not only dries up the springs of the intellectual life, but it shuts off channels of spiritual truth. William Barclay struck a strong and authentic note when he wrote in *The Promise of the Spirit,* "The more a man allows his mind to grow slack and lazy and flabby, the less the Holy Spirit can say to him. True preaching comes when the loving heart and the disciplined mind are laid at the disposal of the Holy Spirit."[1]

In a little book entitled *Prayer and Preaching,* Karl Barth wrote: "The preacher has no right to rely on the Holy Spirit in matters for which he is responsible, without making any effort himself. With all modesty and

[1] (Philadelphia: The Westminster Press, 1960), p. 98.

earnestness he must labour and strive to present the Word aright, even though he is fully aware that only the Holy Spirit can in fact 'teach aright.' "[2]

Another reminds us that "we cannot expect the Spirit's help to teach us what only laziness and personal indifference hinder us from learning; and to despise a power which He gave us capacities to possess is not the way to show that we trust him who gave it."[3] Diligent pursuit of study actually honors the God of all truth and the Spirit of truth.

We know, of course, that "disciple" and "discipline" come from the same root, and both have reference to learning. "Every scribe," said Jesus, "which is [properly] instructed unto the kingdom of heaven is like unto a man that is an householder, which bringeth forth out of his treasure things new and old" (Matt. 13:52). Bishop Hogue long ago pointed out that this is possible only as the scribe keeps putting new things into his treasure. Otherwise, all that comes out will soon be old. The soul is not really on the altar until the mind is there. If the heart be truly dedicated to God, so is the head. "When the minister stops studying, he simply stops!"[4]

What we are talking about is not necessarily formal education, however much that may help. It is still true that "you can lead a boy to college [or seminary], but you can't make him think." It is always easier to get through an educational institution than it is to acquire what education is supposed to represent. As one writer of doggerel has it:

[2](Naperville, Ill.: SCM Book Club, 1964), p. 83.

[3]James Kennedy, *Minister's Shop-Talk* (New York: Harper and Row, 1965), p. 49.

[4]Roy Pearson, *The Ministry of Preaching* (New York: Harper and Brothers, 1959), p. 78.

He's working his way through college,
A task that is awesome and grim—
But a cinch to the job the college has
In working its way through him!

Some of the most effective ministers in the history of the Church have been largely self-educated men. But they have been men who learned to use what they had. They have been men who cultivated an appetite for the books and the parchments.

"Men who die mentally in the ministry," Bishop Kennedy said, "are not murdered—they commit suicide."[5] Milo Arnold wrote in his challenging little volume, *The Adventure of the Christian Ministry,* "A minister must have an insatiable curiosity. If he does not, he will never plumb the depth of the vocation nor venture into the far reaches of his field. There are those who say that a minister loses his effectiveness after he reaches a given age, but it would be better to say he loses his effectiveness when he ceases to wonder. In fact some men, being unable to follow a holy inquisitiveness, have discovered that the ministry was no place for them. The minister who becomes content with what he has discovered of truth will starve both himself and those who look to him for spiritual food."[6]

This is, of course, also the counsel of the ages. On different occasions, John Wesley urged his preachers to constancy and diligence in study. While there may be some adjustment of the time schedule he would set up, there can be no obscuring the high ideal he held for his Methodist ministers as students. Of reading he said,

[5]"We Never Had It So Good," *Pulpit Digest,* XL, No. 261 (January, 1960), 15.

[6](Kansas City, Mo.: Beacon Hill Press of Kansas City, 1967), p. 50.

"Steadily spend all morning in this employ, or at least five hours in the four and twenty. . . . The work of grace would die out in one generation, if the Methodists were not a reading people."[7] Again, Mr. Wesley advised, "Read the most useful books, and that regularly and constantly. . . . If you read no book but the Bible, then you have got above St. Paul. He wanted others too. 'Bring the books,' says he, 'but especially the parchments,' those wrote on parchment. 'But I have no taste for reading' (you say). Contract a taste for it by use, or return to your trade."[8]

In a letter to John Trembath in August of 1760, Wesley wrote:

> What has exceedingly hurt you in time past, nay, and I fear to this day, is want of reading. I scarce ever knew a preacher (to) read so little. And perhaps by neglecting it you have lost the taste for it. Hence your talent in preaching does not increase. It is just the same as it was seven years ago. It is lively, but not deep; there is little variety; there is no compass of thought. Reading only can supply this, with meditation and daily prayer. You wrong yourself greatly by omitting this. You can never be a deep preacher without it any more than a thorough Christian. . . . It is for your life; there is no other way; else you will be a trifler all your days, and a pretty, superficial preacher.[9]

Charles Haddon Spurgeon, virtually a self-educated man, in his lectures to the students of his London ministerial college, said:

> Ignorance of theology is no rare thing in our pulpits, and the wonder is not that so few men are extempore

[7]Quoted, Barclay, *Fishers of Men,* p. 17.

[8]Quoted, Phillip Watson, *The Message of the Wesleys* (New York: The Macmillan Co., 1964), p. 184.

[9]Letter to John Trembath, Aug. 17, 1760; quoted by Watson, *op. cit.,* p. 183-84.

> speakers, but that so many are, when theologians are so scarce. We shall never have great preachers till we have great divines. You cannot build a man-of-war out of a currant bush, nor can great soul-moving preachers be formed out of superficial students. If you would be fluent, that is to say flowing, be filled with all knowledge, especially the knowledge of Christ Jesus your Lord.[10]

Gene Bartlett recalls that many years ago Professor Bruce of Glasgow University, while visiting in the States, heard Phillips Brooks preach on three occasions. His comment was revealing: "Most preachers take to the pulpit a bucketful or half full of the word of God and pump it out to the congregation; but this man is a great watermain, attached to the everlasting reservoir of truth, and a stream of life pours through him by heavenly gravitation to refresh weary souls."[11] Such a situation does not just happen. It comes only as the mind is kept supple and alert by constant grappling with truth.

The preacher's personal intellectual growth depends upon the disciplines of the study. The expansion of knowledge in our day is almost beyond comprehension. To keep in touch with even the periphery is a task almost beyond us. In his own field, the minister dare not be less alert or less well-informed than the laymen to whom he preaches and with whom he counsels. Jaroslav Pelikan asks a serious question at this point: "Does anyone seriously argue that in the church of the future we can afford to have a highly trained laity and a poorly trained ministry, or that the intellectual demands of being a Christian clergyman in the last third of this

[10]Quoted by Thielicke, *op. cit.*, p. 182.

[11]*Op. cit.*, p. 23.

century are less rigorous than they have been in previous times or than they will be for Christian laymen?"[12]

II

The minister must use his study as a battleground on which to face his own doubts and intellectual problems. Certainly he dare not do it in the pulpit. One writer speaks to this point:

> If we hide our doubts from others, we must not hide them from ourselves. We must face them, for only so shall we get the better of them. We must track them to their source. If they are genuinely intellectual doubts we must try to get the measure of them by study and by taking counsel with those more experienced or more learned. If they arise from some sin of pride or neglect, we must seek forgiveness and submit ourselves to spiritual discipline. If they are the effect of suffering we must take firm hold upon the fact that many before us have passed through darkness into new light and a surer knowledge of God. "I had heard of thee with the hearing of the ear, but now mine eye seeth thee." But even in agony of spirit we must go on preaching and wait for God. George Eliot, speaking of Savonarola, says that everybody who has to speak to the crowd must sometimes speak in virtue of yesterday's faith hoping that it will come back tomorrow. Thank God, it generally does![13]

Not for himself alone, but to aid those to whom he ministers, must the preacher grapple with the great questions of faith and life in the modern world. This is not to plead for sophistry or easy answers that do not really meet the questions. Nor is it to deny that some of the questions themselves are phony, while others

[12]*The Christian Intellectual* (New York: Harper and Row, 1965), p. 124.

[13]Leslie J. Tizard, *Preaching: The Art of Communication* (New York: Oxford University Press, 1959), p. 29.

actually have no answers. Mullen says, "His education will not in itself make him an effective minister, but his lack of it may very well keep him from being one. If he is not prepared intellectually for his task, he will be unable to guide persons whose intellectual difficulties stand between them and spiritual growth."[14]

Out of the minister's study must come a gospel with a positive note. In fact, nothing short of this can really be the gospel. On the occasion of the installation of C. E. Macartney to his pulpit in Pittsburgh, Francis L. Patton wrote to the church: "The new minister of your church will come with a message and not a query, and will be fully conscious that zeal in the pulpit will never grow out of doubt in the study."[15] And William Barclay more recently said, "Preaching is therefore the proclamation of certainties, and the confirmation of be-lief. Preaching is designed, not to produce questions, but to answer questions; preaching is designed, not to awaken doubts, but to settle and to conquer doubts. . . . 'Tell me of your certainties,' said Goethe. 'I have doubts enough of my own.' "[16]

III

Some measure of scholarship is the best safeguard against a pulpit ministry that hobbies on one line of truth to the neglect of others. Again Spurgeon, with his usual penchant for vivid illustration, puts the truth before us: "Do not insist perpetually upon one truth

[14]*Op. cit.*, p. 106.

[15]J. Clyde Henry quotes in the introduction to Clarence E. Macartney, *Autobiography: The Making of a Minister* (Great Neck, N.Y.: Channel Press, Inc., 1961), p. 20.

[16]*The Mind of Saint Paul* (New York: Harper and Brothers, 1958), pp. 137-38.

alone. A nose is an important feature in the human countenance, but to paint a man's nose alone is not a satisfactory method of taking his likeness: a doctrine may be very important, but an exaggerated estimate of it may be fatal to a harmonious and complete ministry. Do not make minor doctrines main points. Do not paint the details of the background of the gospel picture with the same heavy brush as the great objects in the foreground of it."[17]

Daniel Niles offers a sobering supposition: "Suppose someone in a congregation kept a record of the sermons preached to that congregation Sunday by Sunday, and then at the end of a whole year wrote a summary of the Christian faith on the basis of those sermons alone, what would that summary contain? Most Christians, among those who attend public worship, live on the basis of the faith they learn on Sunday mornings. The preacher has no right to waste a Sunday morning talking 'tidbits.' "[18]

Scholarship, says Thomas Keir, "is an apparatus for bringing out the truth of Scripture and thus safeguarding the Church against all that is not of Christ. It is one of the means of conditioning the mouth-piece to speak the Word of the eternal God."[19]

Trueblood points out the growing need for sound ministerial scholarship:

> At the same time that a pastor is a teacher in the community, he must also be a scholar. That this follows

[17]Quoted in Thielicke, *op. cit.*, p. 192.

[18]Quoted by Stephen Neill, ed., *Twentieth Century Christianity*
[17]Quoted in Thielicke, *op. cit.*, p. 192.
1963), p. 404.

[19]*The Word in Worship* (London: Oxford University Press, 1962), p. 128.

> necessarily from the recognition of minority status is obvious. Because every item of the Christian view of life is now under violent attack, the attack must be met. The people to meet it are the religious leaders who are liberated from secular earning in order to permit them to engage deeply in the struggle. Every day there are public attacks on the being of God, on the objectivity of the moral order, and on the value of the Church. If these attacks are not met, the battle is lost by default and the majority of Christians becomes utterly confused. The Christian must learn to outthink all opposition. That this is possible is demonstrated by the long history of the Christian faith which has met, in other centuries, attacks quite as strong as those encountered now. But thinking is hard work and we must have men who are prepared to engage in it.[20]

IV

The minister as a student seeks continually for better ways of making known to others the "unsearchable riches of Christ." The preacher's whole life-purpose, as one has said, "is to make the word of God clear and compelling enough to change the lives of men. God expects of His ministers their utmost in preparation—often this means agonizing over what to say and the clearest way to say it. If they do their best, God will give to that best an added insight, power, and blessing, but only if it is their best. The minister as preacher is charged with overcoming the human gospel of despair by the Christian gospel of hope, and he is constantly being forced to stretch his limited talents to their utmost in order to face, and help others to confront, the world and its ideas as they are today."[21] "How we shall present Christ to a constantly changing world is a ques-

[20]*Op. cit.*, p. 47.

[21]James Kennedy, *op. cit.*, p. 68.

tion which should engage us to the end of our ministry."[22]

It is no easy task to be simple without being silly. Our ideal should be that expressed by John Wesley in his oft quoted statements: "I design plain truth for plain people; therefore, of set purpose I abstain from all nice and philosophical speculations; from all perplexed and intimate reasonings; and, as far as possible, from even the show of learning. I labour to avoid all words which are not easy to understand, all which are not used in common life; and, in particular, those kinds of technical terms that so frequently occur in Bodies of Divinity; those modes of speaking which men of reading are intimately acquainted with, but which to the common people are an unknown tongue." "Clearness in particular is necessary for you and for me, because we are to instruct people of the lowest understanding. Therefore we above all, if we think with the wise, yet must speak with the vulgar. We should constantly use the most common, little, easy words (so they are pure and proper) which our language affords."[23]

In similar vein William Barclay adds, "We should use in preaching, in scripture and in worship the best and the simplest language of our own day and generation. It may be that we who have been born and bred in the Church love the old cadences, but are we going to be selfish enough to demand what we sentimentally like while there are millions outside to whom religion will never become a living reality until it talks to them in the language of the common people?"[24]

[22]Bishop Goodwin Hudson at the World Congress on Evangelism, Berlin, West Germany, November 2, 1966.

[23]Quoted by Barclay, *Fishers of Men,* p. 102.

[24]*Ibid.,* p. 104.

This means keeping in touch with real people in real situations. Bishop Gerald Kennedy recalls that John Wesley and one of his preachers came upon two women quarreling near Billingsgate. Their language was forceful if not polite. The preacher suggested that they walk on, but Wesley checked him: "Stay, Sammy, stay, and learn to preach!" "Woe to us," said the bishop, "when we withdraw to our closets and converse only with our own kind."[25]

Another Kennedy, James, claims that "how the minister faces the world often defines the limits of his ministry, for if he ignores the passing scene and attempts to live in the past, or in an unreal, nonexistent present, or in some imaginary future, he fails God, himself, his people, and his world."[26] And David Hubbard, president of Fuller Theological Seminary, said in similar vein, "A minister behind the times may be a menace rather than a blessing to his flock."[27]

Part of the preacher's unremitting intellectual task is to be a translator of the gospel into the idiom and thought patterns of his day. Argentine's Alejandro Clifford has expressed the fear that "conservative evangelicals are losing many of their young people who refuse to accept outmoded traditions expressed in archaic language, and which, though orthodox, seem to have little relevance for life in the twentieth century."[28]

In William Hordern's happy phrase, note it well that the preacher is to be a translator, not a transformer of the gospel.[29] He is not to change its content but

[25]*For Preachers and Other Sinners,* p. 4.

[26]*Op. cit.,* p. 3.

[27]*Bulletin,* Fuller Theological Seminary, April, 1966.

[28]At the World Congress on Evangelism, October 30, 1966.

[29]*New Directions in Theology Today,* Volume I, Introduction (Philadelphia: The Westminster Press, 1966), pp. 141 ff.

to interpret and apply it. He actually needs to be heard. As Trueblood put it in *The Incendiary Fellowship,* "What the professional minister needs to face continually is the sobering fact that he does no good if he is not heard. And hearing is much more than the mere possession of ears. All great tasks, such as those of physicians and lawmakers, require unrelenting imaginative attention, but there is no task in the world which is more demanding in this regard than is the task of the servant of a Christian congregation. Certainly it is not a task for the lazy or the easygoing, whose desire is to have a comfortable life."[30]

"Religious vocabulary," says C. E. Autrey, "changes with each generation, as does the vocabulary of every other field of knowledge. When religion loses its romance and spiritual vitality, it falls into disintegration and is characterized by out-dated language. George F. Sweazey says it 'tries to get along on the stale vocabulary of the last revival.' Terms and expressions which were understood in the nineteenth century may be vague and meaningless in our day. It is essential to evangelism that its motives be clear and expressed in the language of this generation."[31] "The vernacular is the real test," said the late C. S. Lewis. "If you can't turn your faith into it, then either you don't understand it or you don't believe it."[32]

Let it be said again, there must be no reduction of the content and claim of the gospel in this inevitable process of putting it into the language wherein our hearers were born. To paraphrase what Jaroslav Pelikan

[30]P. 51.

[31]*The Theology of Evangelism* (Nashville: Broadman Press, 1966), p. 28.

[32]Quoted by J. A. Davison, "Rehabilitating the Sermon," *Church Management,* June, 1966, p. 7.

wrote about the apologetic needed in our day: "If the preacher is to be heard, he must be able to speak the language of his hearers. But if he is to be worth hearing, he must differentiate himself sufficiently from his setting to stand over against it and to address it." Pelikan further speaks of an "apologetic by abdication" which he says is able to "speak to its culture only by reducing the content of its message." Such, he points out, is doomed to failure; for it will remove layer after layer of its tradition, in response to one objection or another, until there is no significant continuity left between it and the evangel in whose name it claims to speak."[33]

To purchase so-called "relevance" at the cost of anything significant to say is obviously to pay too high a price. There is wisdom in Vance Havner's comment that "the very fact that men cannot endure sound doctrine is all the more reason for seeing that they get it. It is not our responsibility to make it acceptable; it is our duty to make it available."[34]

Dr. Billy Graham likewise warns against changing Christianity into a new humanism by succumbing to the "growing pressure to accommodate the Christian message to minds and hearts darkened by sin—to give precedence to the material and physical need, while distorting the spiritual need, which is basic to every person."[35]

Lutheran Theologian William Hordern raises the question "whether 'modern man,' however we define him, is so impressive that we must transform the Christian faith to suit him. Is modern man still the old-fashioned sinner dressed up in a space suit? Are the unbelievers of today, like the unbelievers of Paul's day,

[33]*Op. cit.,* pp. 25, 33-34.

[34]*Pepper 'n Salt* (Westwood, N.J.: Fleming H. Revell Company, 1966), p. 29.

[35]At the World Congress on Evangelism, October 26, 1966.

'blinded by the god of this passing age'? (II Cor. 4:4, NEB)."

Hordern also recalls that Karl Barth has challenged us to ask whether it is the Christian gospel or modern man who is irrelevant. Barth, he says, "suggests that our problem is not with a world come of age but with 'a world which *regards* itself as of age (and proves daily that it is precisely not that).' (*The Humanity of God*, pp. 58-9). In such a situation, Barth says that it is dangerous to approach modern man 'with some sort of gibberish, which, for the moment, is modern,' because what we have to say both to other men and to ourselves 'is a strange piece of news.' The important thing to see is that it is also 'the *great* piece of news.' To translators it appears that the gospels of the transformers have lost all greatness. They are acceptable to modern man precisely because they do not challenge him deeply. Such 'radical theology' turns out to be nothing more than a slightly theological expression of what is heard on all sides today."[36]

V

This means that the preacher will cultivate a broad base of reading and study. I quote with approval, on occasion, John Wesley's statement in the preface to his *Standard Sermons*, "Let me be a man of one book." What he meant, very obviously, was not that he would read and study only the Bible, but that the Bible would be the Touchstone and unifying Core about which all his other extremely broad reading would be integrated. Dwight Stevenson wrote, "A man who studies only one book does not even understand that book. This is because God loves the whole world and works seven days

[36]*Op. cit.*, pp. 151-52.

a week, not merely on Sunday. The whole realm of culture and learning is his concern. A man who is sheltered from the yearning, the thoughts, and the hungers of the world is ill-equipped to serve a Master who loved publicans and sinners. In creative literature at its best—that is, in biography, drama, short story, and novels—there 'cross the crowded ways of life,' and one hears 'the cries of race and clan.' There he may not learn what God's action may be, but he will come closer to man's need."[37]

The study must never become a refuge from reality. Milo Arnold warns us that "a man who finds it difficult to encounter people may excuse himself from the painful task of calling by burying his head in a book. Books are dangerous things if they become hiding places."[38]

Books may also be a snare if the preacher becomes a man of thoughts, rather than a man of thought. Oliver Wendell Holmes once said that, while a man may milk 300 cows, he should make his own butter.

VI

The preacher will never become or remain the student he should be without a time budget as moment-pinching as his money budget is necessarily of his pennies. The mere fact of a budget does not, obviously, make either more money or more moments. As someone wrote:

Budgeting is the thing to do;
On that I'm most emphatic.
I'm just as broke as I ever was,
But now it's systematic.

[37]*The False Prophet* (New York: Abingdon Press, 1965), p. 89.

[38]*Op. cit.*, p. 77.

Wayne Oates writes, "All that a minister has to give away is time. He should do this with more skill than that with which businessmen give away, invest, and earn dividends on money. A flexible, shrewd use of time is necessary to the minister's own health as well as to his effectiveness."[39] And Arnold reminds us, "A few ministers have failed because they didn't know enough. Some ministers have failed because they didn't pray enough. Possibly some clergymen have failed because they lacked talent. But the number is legion who have accomplished less than they could, or should, because of the poor use of time."[40]

In an article entitled "Fresh Out of Boot Camp," Claude Garrison, a Methodist minister and former district superintendent, wrote concerning the importance of the disciplined use of time:

> The young man is inclined to flee from strict discipline upon graduation from school, hoping he will never again hear another class bell ring. But what he accepted as routine in the halls of learning must be assumed with dignity and gladness in the pastorate. Never will he become effective unless and until he rings his own class bells, makes his own assignments, and devises a scheduled routine that will afford him the satisfaction of getting work done on schedule without allowing it to become mere routine.
>
> The unscheduled, unplanned day is entirely too common. The man who fails here tends to have no rigid schedule of sermon preparation, slight faithfulness to regular reading. He is spasmodic in parish visitation and is not very accountable in matters of administration. In its extreme form the man becomes a problem to himself, to his church, and to his family.[41]

[39]*The Minister's Own Mental Health* (Great Neck, N.Y.: Channel Press, Inc., 1961), p. 16.

[40]*Op. cit.*, p. 47.

[41]*Christian Advocate,* September 13, 1962, p. 10.

The time budget should be realistic. It must certainly be flexible. But it will save the preacher from working against himself—thinking while in prayer that he should be calling, or while calling that he should be studying, or while studying that he should be working on midweek mailers. No man can stand working with a perpetually guilty conscience.

Within the time set aside for study, it is important to develop a purposeful program. That there will be study directly for sermon preparation goes without saying. But beyond the immediate task of preparing to preach the next sermon, there should be a systematic program of general study and reading. The minister will study books about preaching, about counselling and church administration. He will read books of sermons, less for specific outlines than for seed thoughts and usable illustrations. He will need to read the holiness literature, classic and current; and books on theology and the philosophy of religion. Basic to all will be a systematic plan of Bible study that should over the years develop an increasing, firsthand knowledge of all the Word of God.

There will be a certain amount of free reading. "Reading maketh a full man," is Francis Bacon's well-known aphorism. Almost anything in the way of history, literature, biography, science both popular and more technical, travel, and current events will prove to be grist for the preacher's mill if he reads with notebook or pad at hand and with alert mind.

Important in this connection is a system to preserve the fruits of study. It may be in the nature of notebooks or a filing system. I have no particular pet idea to sell. The only thing is, it should be simple and one that a busy preacher can live with. A friend of mine bought a ready-made system, far overpriced, it seemed to me.

When I asked him later how he liked it, he said, "It's wonderful—if you have a full-time secretary to keep it up."

A sermon seedbed is a significant part of every preacher's study program. The best sermons are those that grow, not those built under the pressure of a preaching deadline. Most sermons start with a text or topic, to which divisions, content material, and illustrations may be readily added.

At this point also, let me put in a plug for a long-range preaching plan. While my personal preference would be for one based on a section of Scripture, almost any plan is better than none at all. For one thing, the preacher will pick up material on topics to be treated at a later date almost without effort while in study or reading on other themes. Claude Garrison, again, said, "If the Holy Spirit is to have opportunity to lead us, we must seek audience with Him through real work sessions behind closed doors, using the tools we possess. Once you pay the price of making a plan of preaching for the church year, you will never turn back. Every week, while doing many different things and reading from many different sources, you will come upon materials and you will say to yourself, 'I've got a sermon coming up on that.' Under this plan it is easy to have some things on the way without having the homiletical axe out all the time trying frantically to chop wood for the very next sermon."[42]

A further advantage of a preaching plan is one already alluded to under the values of disciplined study in general. William Barclay explains:

> Unless the preacher systematically plans, he will continue to preach on those things which mean most to him and those things which are in the forefront of his

[42]*Ibid.*

> mind. When this happens you get unbalanced preaching. We know for instance the kind of preacher who preaches the second coming in season and out of season. We know the pacifist who cannot keep pacifism out of his sermons. We know the kind of preacher who does nothing but thunder denunciation and the kind of preacher who does nothing but preach an almost sentimentalized love. To whom, we must add the preacher who is all *Honest to God,* or all religion and politics. If we preach only about the things we want to preach about, we will necessarily preach a sadly truncated gospel.[43]

If all of this has made the ministry seem like hard brainwork and no business for a lazy mind, that is all to the good. It doesn't take brilliance or superabundance of personality, but it does take honesty and faithfulness in the full use and development of the talents God has given each of us. That our calling also demands of us a true piety and deep spirituality does not make its intellectual requirements the less but even the more exacting. As Elton Trueblood expressed it, "In the Church, even more than in the world, it is important that each task be done well rather than clumsily, because there is so much at stake. The Christian writer must discipline himself to write clearly, and the Christian speaker must discipline himself to speak convincingly. The fact that we are dealing with holy things does not mean that piety can take the place of costly competence."[44]

In closing, consider the lines of "The Teacher's Prayer," written by Handley C. G. Moule, himself a scholar of the first rank:

Lord and Saviour, true and kind,
Be the Master of my mind;
Bless and guide, and strengthen still,
All my powers of thought and will.

[43]*Fishers of Men,* pp. 107-8.
[44]*Op. cit.,* pp. 113-14.

While I ply the scholar's task,
Jesus Christ, be near, I ask;
Help the memory, clear the brain,
Knowledge still to seek and gain.

Thou hast made me, mind and soul;
I for Thee would use the whole.
Thou hast died that I might live;
All my powers to Thee I give.

Striving, thinking, learning still,
Let me follow then Thy will,
Till my whole glad nature be
Trained for duty and for Thee.

CHAPTER 4

The Minister as Preacher

In its broadest terms, preaching is the oral communication of the gospel. As such, it is the Christian minister's chief task, his supreme work. Neglect at this point can never be made up anywhere else. As Emil Brunner once put it: "Where there is true preaching, where, in the obedience of faith, the Word is proclaimed, there, in spite of all appearances to the contrary, the most important thing that ever happens upon this earth takes place."[1]

After all has been said for other modes of communication, preaching is still the chief way God reaches human hearts with His redemptive truth. As the translator of Helmut Thielicke's *The Trouble with the Church* has said in the preface to this volume, "Wherever we find, even in this day, a vital, living congregation, we find at its center vital preaching." And Elton Trueblood, who quotes these words, adds, "There have been no changes in our culture which alter the fact that the

[1]*Revelation and Reason*, p. 142; quoted, Bartlett, *op. cit.*, p. 38.

spoken word may be a powerful force in human life. Good preaching is still possible and sometimes it makes a crucial difference. Though the time when it was easy to assemble a crowd is over, at least for the immediate present, it is still true that people will gather where they have reason to believe that something will be said, with clarity and conviction, about life's most important issues."[2]

The challenge of our times is not chiefly for more preaching. It is definitely for better preaching. Gordon H. Clark, writing in *Contemporary Evangelical Thought,* says: "If Christianity instead of its modern imitations is to make an impact on our society, preaching must become richer, fuller, and more profound. And in addition, the faith that is preached should be defended against the attacks of its enemies by the formulation and exposition of a thoroughly biblical world-view. This requires more scholars, more discussion, more publication, and a wider appreciation of the importance of the task."[3]

The purpose of preaching is to relate the Word of God to the needs of men. It is to build a bridge between the saving truth and the person to be saved.[4] Faris Whitesell wrote: "The preacher should be able to feel the pulse and sense the mood of the age in which he lives. To do this, he must be in touch with the currents of life and thought. Such understanding will help him slant his preaching to today's world rather than to yesterday's. Luccock says that ours is an age with a sense of insignificance, insecurity, anxiety, futility, emptiness. Others call it a bewildered age where we live in a

[2]*Op. cit.,* p. 48.

[3]Carl F. H. Henry, editor (Great Neck, N.Y.: Channel Press, 1957), p. 161.

[4]Cf. Bartlett, *op. cit.,* p. 54.

moral vacuum. Objective, valid moral standards are almost a thing of the past. What an age in which to preach the eternally fixed moral truths of divine revelation as revealed in expository preaching!"[5]

Robert Mounce defines preaching as "that timeless link between God's great redemptive Act and man's apprehension of it. It is the medium through which God contemporizes His historic Self-disclosure and offers man the opportunity to respond in faith. Without response, revelation is incomplete. Without preaching, God's mighty act remains an event in the past. What man desperately needs is a redemptive encounter in the ever present Now. Preaching answers to this need by contemporizing the past and moving the individual to respond in faith."[6]

In preaching, God, who is eternal, utters His "solving and saving Word in the situation that is contemporary."[7] John R. W. Stott said, "It is by preaching that God makes past history a present reality. The cross was, and will always remain, a unique historical event of the past. And there it will remain, in the past, in the books, unless God himself makes it real and relevant to men today. It is by preaching, in which He makes His appeal to men through men, that God accomplishes this miracle. He opens their eyes to see its true meaning, its eternal value and its abiding merit."[8] And Paul Scherer adds the thought that "the Bible is the preacher's book, not simply because it is the story of what happened once,

[5]*Power in Expository Preaching* (Westwood, N.J.: Fleming H. Revell Co., 1963), p. 134.

[6]*The Essential Nature of New Testament Preaching* (Grand Rapids: Wm. B. Eerdmans Publishing Co., 1960), p. 153.

[7]Keir, *op. cit.*, p. 121.

[8]*Op. cit.*, p. 53.

but also because in it and through it and by way of it that very thing is happening now."[9]

If preaching is as important an element in the minister's total task as we have come to believe it is, there should be—and there is—much in the New Testament about it. It is our purpose to look at some of the ways in which true preaching is described. A list of seven great terms describe the function of preaching as fulfilled by the minister in his roles of messenger, voice, apostle, herald, prophet, evangelist, and teacher.

I

The first and probably most important single term for preaching in the New Testament is *kerussein,* which means to announce as a herald, to proclaim a message. It is used some 38 times in the New Testament, almost half of them in the Gospels. Paul uses it 13 times, as in I Cor. 1:23-24, "We preach [proclaim] Christ crucified, unto the Jews a stumblingblock, and unto the Greeks foolishness; but unto them which are called, both Jews and Greeks, Christ the power of God, and the wisdom of God." It is translated "preach, proclaim, publish," and the corresponding noun *kerux* or "herald," is always translated "preacher." From it is derived the familiar term *kerygma,* a proclamation, now used in New Testament studies as a technical term for the proclamation of the gospel to the world.

This term has been described as "a parable in one word." It pictures the preacher as a herald riding through the city, calling men to arms, proclaiming an amnesty from the king, speaking boldly in the name of

[9]*The Word God Sent* (New York: Harper and Row, 1965), p. 77.

the monarch.[10] It emphasizes the fact that the Christian preacher speaks as a messenger, making a proclamation he did not originate, telling the good news of what Another has done. Lawrence Toombs says, "Metaphysical sermons, designed to expose the mystery of the divine nature, may impress the congregation with the minister's erudition, but they will always fall short of the gospel. Preaching is not an inquisitive poking and prying into the character of God, but a proclamation of what God has done with his people Israel and for mankind in Jesus Christ."[11]

In similar vein, George Buttrick has written: "Preaching is not the airing of our opinions on books or history or even on Jesus. It is not a lecture on religion. It is not 'The Christian Interpretation of Life.' It is not even a homily on the Christian religion. It is . . . the declaration of an Event, without which there could be no Christian interpretations of life. It is not the utterance of our conviction, but of the happening which seizes and seals our conviction. . . . The gospel is the heralding of something already done for men, the *annunciation of a fact* so staggering in joy that Browning's Clean had some right to say of the early Christians, 'Their doctrines could be held by no sane man.' Their preacher is one who breaks in upon his fellowmen crying, 'The most wonderful thing has happened.' "[12]

Whatever else it means, and it does mean much more, proclaiming what God has done in Christ imparts the note of authority to the preacher's word. He speaks

[10]Jesse Burton Weatherspoon, *Sent Forth to Preach* (New York: Harper and Brothers, 1954), p. 62.

[11]*The Old Testament in Christian Preaching* (Philadelphia: The Westminster Press, 1961), p. 61.

[12]Quoted, Weatherspoon, *op. cit.,* p. 92.

with all the weight of the King whose herald he is. People today indeed long to hear an authoritative word —that word which comes as the word of God. More proclamation and less denunciation will still be the positive preaching that grips and holds the modern mind.[13]

II

A second term for preaching comes from the Greek word for "gospel"—*euangelizein.* It is the source of our English words evangelize, evangelism, evangelistic and means, literally, to bring, announce, or tell good or glad tidings. The noun representing the content of the action is "gospel," the good news. The noun representing the one speaking is "evangelist." It is closely related to proclamation in that it has particular reference to the Christian message for a lost world.

The priority of evangelism in the preaching ministry of the Church is seen in the fact that the great word for the Church's message—the word gospel—is the very term from which *evangelism* comes. Evangelism is not just *part* of the Church's task in the world. It comes very close to being the *whole* of it. It was to one who filled what we would call a pastoral office that Paul wrote the injunction, "Do the work of an evangelist" (II Tim. 4:5).

D. T. Niles has written, "Evangelism is the struggle for the salvation of this world. It is the continuation of the ministry of the Incarnate God who came that the world might be redeemed."[14] Jesus came "to seek and to save that which was lost" (Luke 19:10), and His word

[13]With apologies to P. T. Forsyth, *Positive Preaching and the Modern Mind.*

[14]*The Preacher's Task and the Stone of Stumbling* (New York: Harper and Brothers, 1958), p. 34.

to His disciples was, "As my Father hath sent me, even so send I you" (John 20:21; cf. 17:18). That which had so large a place in the work of the Early Church must have an important place in ours.

Jesse Weatherspoon, in his excellent volume entitled *Sent Forth to Preach,* wrote: "The consciousness of having been divinely called to participate with Christ in his redemptive mission as heralds of the gospel; an eager openness to the power and guidance of the Holy Spirit; a broad and lofty conception of preaching as an effective method of winning men to faith; and the possession of a message that burned in their minds and hearts as the only hope of the world's salvation—these are facts of apostolic evangelism that are fundamental for all who would strengthen and make permanent the new evangelism that gives promise of so much."[15]

Leighton Ford recalls the analogy used by Samuel Zwemer, the great missionary to the Islamic world: "Evangelism is a collision of souls. We may measure its effect by an equation: mv = i or mass times velocity equals impact. If we let *mass* stand for the truth of the Gospel," Mr. Ford says, "then the *impact* of our Gospel on the world will be in direct proportion to the *velocity* —the *urgency*—with which it is delivered."[16]

There is a caution we should not forget in Halford Luccock's reminder that "a live church is seeking out sinners; the real calamity for a church occurs when it becomes full of 'nice' people on a 'nice' street in a 'nice' part of town. A nice little church can never be of much use in the work of the kingdom of God."[17]

[15]P. 103.

[16]*Op. cit.,* p. 13.

[17]"Simeon Stylites," *Christian Century,* LXXVII, No. 11 (March 16, 1960), 335.

But there is one other point we must not overlook in connection with preaching as evangelizing. It is preaching that must be characterized by love and joy. "The preaching which is all threat and no love may terrify, but it will not save."[18]

Free Methodist Bishop J. Paul Taylor wrote in this connection:

> It is easy enough for one lacking the fullness of joy to lash out with legalistic sternness against devotees of the world's pleasures, forgetting that the world is an unhappy, hungry world. Majoring in ridicule of modern music and dancing, in which a chaos of sound is wedded to madness of movement, is to dig a chasm between oneself and souls desperately needing help, making contact impossible. That is the procedure of the Pharisaical elder brother, who can think of nothing but the wild, wastrel life of his prodigal brother. But all of his severe condemnation does not induce the lost son to take one step away from the swine pen. He is an exceedingly unhappy man who repulses rather than draws, a man who never had a feast for his own soul, and resents the music and dancing and merriment in the Father's house that attracted the prodigal in the "pearl of parables."[19]

The content of the communication itself may be altered by the manner and spirit in which it is uttered. The very tone of one's voice may make a great difference in what actually gets through to others. Scotland's George Duncan said at the World Congress on Evangelism in Berlin:

> I believe that the accuracy of the message must be secured and safeguarded, not only in a careful presentation of the truth of God . . . but also by careful regard

[18]William Barclay, *Corinthians: Daily Bible Study* (Philadelphia: The Westminster Press, 1956), p. 131.

[19]*Holiness, the Finished Foundation* (Winona Lake, Ind.: Light and Life Press, 1963), pp. 112-13.

> to the tone of voice we may use. It is just as possible to distort and misrepresent the grace and mercy of God in Christ by the tone of voice with which we address our people as it is to distort the truth of the Gospel as revealed in Christ by the error we may proclaim. We are told of Christ himself that He was "full of grace and truth"; one feels that Christ would never have used the tone of voice one so often hears today.
>
> I remember very vividly passing among the back streets of London, and seeing a young Christian preaching in the open air to a crowd of bystanders. He held in his hand a big Bible but I felt he should have held a big stick, for he was simply flogging the people. As I listened to his voice I found myself asking, "Would Jesus Christ ever have spoken like that?" . . . This young man's presentation of God's grace was wrecked and ruined by how he presented the truth.[20]

One of the saddest of all the mistakes attributed to William Archibald Spooner of Oxford, from whom we get the term "spoonerisms" for such verbal errors, was his speaking of "the tearful chidings of the gospel" when he meant to say "the cheerful tidings of the gospel."[21]

Perhaps another way of making this point would be to call attention to the Bible's own identification of the mood of its gospel: "Behold, I bring you good tidings of great joy, which shall be to all people. For unto you is born this day in the city of David a Saviour, which is Christ the Lord" (Luke 2:10-11). What we need as much as anything in these days is a revival of the note of praise and joy in preaching. What we have to tell is good news. It may and does involve the note of judgment. Yet the underlying tone of the preacher's message should reflect the joy of salvation.

Frederick W. Schroeder in *Preaching the Word with Authority* underlines this point: "Making men aware of

[20]November 2, 1966.

[21]William M. Elliott, Jr., *Power to Master Life* (New York: Abingdon Press, 1964), p. 96.

their sin and need is one thing; concentrating on their willfulness and wickedness to the virtual exclusion of the good news of the gospel is something else again. It is the bane of a considerable portion of American preaching that it is excessively analytical. If there is any one thing that most of us do unusually well in the pulpit, it is that of making a thorough analysis of the human situation; in fact, diagnosis has become so much a commonplace in preaching that the pulpit is said to suffer from the paralysis of analysis."[22]

Bishop Taylor quotes significant words: "We have still to learn the ministry of joy. . . . We know men to be sinful, and we point them—often too unlovingly—to the source of salvation. One thing only we often fail to realize—that men are sad and need joy, that they are discouraged and need hope, that they are stunted and need sunshine. And so we stand by the bedside of sick humanity, measuring out dreary prescriptions and wondering at their scant effect."[23]

German Theologian Paul Deitenbeck quoted Bezzel as saying, "In every sermon should sound forth [the words] . . . 'I rejoice—rejoice with me!' " He added, "In this joy-hungry world people try in all possible ways to manufacture happiness that lasts for only a short time. Lasting joy is found only in Jesus. Therefore God's colaborers can be helpers of joy, since they live in the joy of the Lord. Thus our faith even lends a sense of humor to everyday life. Our little gems of daily joy can make it easier for another to come to Jesus."[24]

The true credentials of our ministry do not hang framed on the wall of the study. They live in the record

[22] (Philadelphia: The Westminster Press, 1954), p. 50.

[23] *Op. cit.*, p. 114.

[24] At the World Congress on Evangelism, November 3, 1966.

of changed lives. "Miracles of grace," said C. H. Spurgeon, "must be the seals of our ministry."[25] The evangelistic passion in preaching, Spurgeon defined as "logic set on fire."[26] "The best way to preach sinners to Christ," he said, "is to preach Christ to sinners."[27]

III

The third term used in the New Testament to describe preaching is one of the most common of Greek verbs—*lalein.* It means to tell, to speak. It is the word used of Jesus in Mark 2:2, "He preached [spoke] the word to them." It is used five times in the Acts with the meaning of preaching (8:25; 11:19; 13:42; 14:25; 16:6). Paul used it of his oral ministry in I Cor. 2:13, "Which things we speak, not in the words which man's wisdom teacheth, but which the Holy Ghost teacheth; comparing spiritual things with spiritual."

This, should we need it, may serve us as a reminder that preaching is the spoken word. One may have a sermon on paper, in his notes, or thought out in advance. But it becomes preaching when and as it is delivered.

The converse, of course, is clear. Speaking implies hearing. This points to the importance of rapport with the congregation. There is a give-and-take in preaching in which the sermon gains in the very act of speaking. Preaching as telling or speaking involves dialogue. Gene Bartlett wrote:

> The *preached* word is also the *heard* word—and each hears with his own experience. The preacher will need to take into account the simple fact that he is engaged not in monologue but in a conversation. At points in his preaching his sermon will need to reflect the reaction

[25]Thielicke, *op. cit.,* p. 71.
[26]*Ibid.,* p. 55.
[27]*Loc. cit.*

> of those to whom he is preaching. This is an important part of the sensitivity of the preacher. He must show that he knows the hearer as well as the word. Not only must he be aware of God's disclosure, but he must also be sensitive to the acceptances and resistances which are in the listener. So the worshiper must feel that in the preacher he too has a voice. He is an active part of the conversation, a subject acting, not an object acted upon.[28]

Possibly as a parenthesis we should note a point Thomas Keir has made. The responsibility upon the preacher to speak implies a responsibility upon the people to hear. "Throughout its entire length the Bible insists on the responsibility, not only of the preacher, but of the *hearer*. . . . There are not only different qualities of preacher but different qualities of *hearer*. 'The people said that it thundered: others said, An angel spake' (John xii.29). . . . The real ages of great preaching have always been the ages of great hearing. It is not possible to say that great preaching is prior to great hearing or vice versa, but only that they closely condition each other."[29]

Preaching as speaking involves directness of discourse. *Lalein* is to speak to or tell to someone. Speaking in the third person is rarely preaching. Unless there is an "I—thou" relationship set up between the preacher and his audience, the communication may be a lecture or an oral essay, but it is not preaching.

Bartlett again reminds us of the difference between simply attracting attention and gaining interest. "Attracting attention may make a man an onlooker, but it does not make him a participant. Real interest comes when one feels himself involved, or to use a better word,

[28]*Op. cit.*, p. 44.
[29]*Op. cit.*, pp. 4-5.

'addressed,' as Martin Buber would put it. This, I think, more than any device or any homiletic skill, is the secret of real interest. We are interested in that which involves us. Let it become clear that a sermon is dealing with the living options which confront a person, and inevitably he becomes interested in the outcome. Disengaged preaching which does not address a person in the living situation inevitably becomes dull because it is irrelevant, dealing with no living options."[30]

Herbert Farmer wrote along the same line: "Good matter, felicitous language, firm structure and arrangement, only become great preaching in proportion as they become, in the way that only speech can, the vehicle of a direct I—thou relationship between you and those you address."[31]

This involves what we have already noted in relation to the minister as a student. He must strive to express his message in simple, plain, forthright language. The preacher who blows a forgotten tune on an uncertain trumpet should not wonder that no one listens.[32]

Martin Luther said, "Sermons should be addressed to the . . . commonality. If in my discourses I were to be thinking about Melancthon and the other doctors I should do no good at all: but I preach in plain language to the plain, unlearned people, and that pleases all parties. If I know the Greek, Hebrew, and Latin languages, I reserve them for our learned meetings, where they are of use, for at these we deal in such subtleties and

[30]*Op. cit.*, p. 51.

[31]*The Servant of the Word* (New York: Charles Scribner's Sons, 1942), p. 51.

[32]Suggested by Robert C. Strom in *Behold a New Thing,* ed. Robert B. Cunningham (Department of Evangelism, United Presbyterian church, n.d.), p. 34.

such profundities, that God Himself, I wot, must sometimes marvel at us."[33]

James Denney's advice is worth following: "Don't preach over people's heads. The man who shoots above the target does not prove thereby that he has superior ammunition. He just proves that he can't shoot."[34]

This does not mean shallowness—"talking down" to people. Preaching down never lifts up. The one thing worse than talking over the heads of the people is not talking to their heads at all. Rather, as John Wesley said, "Preachers may think with the learned, but must speak with the common people."[35] Charles Spurgeon wrote, "It is not enough to be so plain that you can be understood; you must speak so that you cannot be misunderstood. . . . Our speech must be forceful. Some imagine that this consists in speaking loudly, but I can assure them they are in error. Nonsense does not improve by being bellowed."[36]

John Broadus said, "One must habitually think his thoughts into clearness, and must acquire wide and easy command of the best resources of language, if he would be able to speak simply and yet really say something."[37] When we truly understand the nature of preaching as speaking or telling, we shall be a long way up the road from the type of sermon described by the late Andrew

[33]Quoted from *Table Talk,* by Ralph G. Turnbull, *A Minister's Obstacles* (Westwood, N.J.: Fleming H. Revell, 1946), p. 181.

[34]Quoted, Paul S. Rees, *Stir Up the Gift* (Grand Rapids: Zondervan Publishing House, 1952), p. 137.

[35]Quoted; John Broadus, *The Preparation and Delivery of Sermons* (New York: Harper and Brothers, 1926), p. 242.

[36]Quoted, Thielicke, *op. cit.,* p. 91.

[37]***Op. cit.,* p. 276**

W. Blackwood as "an unilluminating discussion of unreal problems in unintelligible language."[38]

IV

A fourth term to be considered, *didaskein,* means to teach, to give instruction, to instruct by means of discourse with others. It is used in this sense 97 times in the New Testament. Two nouns relate to the content of the teaching: *didache* and *didaskalia,* the latter of which "seems more strongly to indicate consistent teaching according to some standard."[39]

Teaching in the New Testament sense, together with other terms we shall examine, comes very close to being what we should today call "pastoral preaching." It must never be set over against "preaching" as if it were something entirely different. It has particular reference to preaching in the church, although it is used in the ministry of Jesus to refer to His public discourses to the multitudes, many of whom were not and never became His disciples. Teaching consolidates the gains of the gospel. It interprets and explains what is being proclaimed. H. Grady Davis says:

> Teaching is not held in lower esteem than preaching in the New Testament church. According to the record, Jesus both preached the kingdom of God and taught concerning it, and we should not doubt that the evangelist means both when he says both. So Peter and Paul and all the rest both preached and taught. Teaching is included in every important listing of a minister's duties in the New Testament.
>
> Teaching, like preaching, is done at God's command and in his name, with the full assurance that he works

[38]*The Fine Art of Preaching* (New York: The Macmillan Co., 1937), p. 30.

[39]H. Grady Davis, *Design for Preaching* (Philadelphia: Fortress Press, 1958), p. 120.

> through it. The teacher, like the preacher, is qualified for his task by direct endowment of the Holy Spirit: teaching is by charismatic gift, like every other function in the body of Christ. Teaching no less than preaching has God for its author and supporter.[40]

Davis points out also that, in the references in the New Testament to the assembly of Christians, the more characteristic forms of speech are described as teaching and prophecy, rather than preaching. Thus in Acts 2:42 the believers are said to have "continued stedfastly in the apostles' doctrine [*didache*] and fellowship, and in breaking of bread, and in prayers." Paul reminded the Corinthians that he had sent Timothy to them to bring them, as he said, "into remembrance of my ways which be in Christ, as I teach everywhere in every church" (I Cor. 4:17).

This verse gives us another important consideration in teaching. It was not only carried on "in every church" but it was concerned with "ways which be in Christ," that is, the Christian ethic. This is in no sense a moralistic endeavor. It is the setting forth of the pattern of life which is implied in acceptance of the gospel proclaimed—the "so what," if you will, of the new life in Christ.

As such, teaching in the public ministry of the Church is not only legitimate but indispensable. As Davis notes, "The great Christian preachers have always been both heralds of the gospel and teachers. Indeed, while proclamation and teaching can be easily distinguished as types of discourse, in practice it is by no means easy to tell where one leaves off and the other begins."[41] The "believing side" and the "behaving side"

[40] *Ibid.*, pp. 120-21.

[41] *Ibid.*, p. 125.

of the Christian faith blend into and are continuous with one another like the two halves of a sphere.

V

Our next term descriptive of preaching in the New Testament is much misunderstood, yet very important. It is *prophetein*—to prophesy. It literally means to speak forth, and in the secular Greek of New Testament times meant interpreting the oracles of the gods.[42] In both the Old Testament and the New, "to prophesy" carried as one of its meanings "to predict or foretell" (cf. John 11:51). However in both the Old Testament and the New, to prophesy meant also to forthtell the will of God, particularly to declare what cannot be known by natural means (e.g., Matt. 26:68). There are, of course, those like W. E. Vine who hold that prophecy as a function of the ministry ceased with the completion of the canon of Scripture.[43] Yet there is a real sense, as Davis points out, in which the gospel is the fulfillment of prophecy, and its preaching is "a continuation of the prophet's work."[44] The prophetic note in the Christian ministry is the forthtelling of the will of God under the direct and immediate anointing of the Holy Spirit.

Paul's statement in I Cor. 14:3 sounds very much like a specification of the meaning of New Testament prophecy: "He that prophesieth speaketh unto men to edification, and exhortation, and comfort." None of these terms imply *de novo* prediction. All of them represent results fully as much needed in the Church now as in New Testament times. Thayer defines the word *prophet* in the New Testament as "one who, moved by the Spirit of God and hence his organ or spokesman, solemnly

[42] *Op. cit.*, III, 221-22.
[43] *Loc. cit.*
[44] *Op. cit.*, p. 109.

declares to men what he has received by inspiration, especially future events, and in particular such as relate to the cause and kingdom of God and to human salvation."[45]

It is significant that the contemporaries of Jesus never thought of Him as a Priest, although He prayed much. They always referred to Him as *rabbi*, Teacher, or as "one of the prophets." They wondered if He were "the prophet that was to come," the eschatological prophet whose appearance would usher in the day of the Lord. It was His ministry of teaching and preaching that earned Him the titles of Rabbi and Prophet.

Prophesying in the Christian sense is "the proclamation of the revealed word of God under the guidance of the Spirit and the interpretation of God's word and God's activity in their moral and spiritual meaning."[46]

There is something of the same distinction between prophet and teacher as we saw in the Old Testament to exist between prophet and priest. E. Stanley Jones points this up when he writes: "In the church of Antioch there were 'prophets and teachers' (Acts 13:1). Teachers are usually the conservators of the past, passing on the lessons that have been learned from the ancestors. Prophets are usually the radicals—they want to apply the lessons of the past to the present and the future. They press the 'Is' into the 'Ought-to-be.' Without them we sink from the 'Is' to the 'Was.' Keep alive the prophet in your soul."[47] "The mission of the prophet is the life-blood of the Church."[48]

Perhaps, as Dwight Stevenson claims, the prophetic

[45]Quoted, *ibid.*, p. 93.

[46]Weatherspoon, *op. cit.*, p. 71.

[47]*Growing Spiritually*, p. 195.

[48]Clifford, *op. cit.*, p. 27.

mood is even more important in our day than in the past. "It is difficult," he says, "even for a man of God, to live in an affluent society without becoming a man of the world. Then the genuine, prophetic function goes out of the ministry, and the minister becomes the twentieth-century counterpart of the town crier, mounting the pulpit every Sunday morning and calling out, 'Eleven o'clock, and all is well!' He cries 'Peace, when there is no peace.' He soothes and solaces when he ought to disturb; he condones when he ought to judge and forgive. The false prophet may be a prophet of Baal."[49] Such preaching fits perfectly the mood of the woman who said, "I want to be moved, not upset!"

What prophecy means to us above all is the anointing of the Holy Spirit, both in guiding us into all truth and in empowering the proclamation of His Word. In F. B. Meyer's glowing comparison, "the Holy Spirit operates as electric power along the wire of the word."[50]

[49]*Op. cit.*, p. 41.

[50]*Expository Preaching Plans and Methods,* pp. 12-13. Cf. also Dr. J. B. Chapman's analogy: "We fear that men sometimes think of abstract truth as possessing power to make new and lead aright, and that they emphasize education to the overshadowing of regeneration and vital religion. Truth in the abstract may be likened to the cable which, while ever so necessary, is cold and lifeless and powerless except the hot, burning, powerful electric current permeate it. But just as the cable which is permeated with the electric current is 'alive,' so also is the truth when accompanied by the Spirit.

"And just as a cable of silver furnishes a much better path for the current than a log of wood, so does clear, definite, biblical doctrine furnish a better channel for the Holy Spirit than doctrine which is mixed with error and misapprehension. But just as a cable of the finest conductibility can do no useful work without the current, so the most flawless orthodoxy can accomplish no genuine work of salvation apart from the Spirit" (*Herald of Holiness,* March 23, 1927, p. 1).

The wire without the power is worthless. One of another generation still speaks to an all-important point when he says, "No man can do the Christian work of witnessing for and of Christ without that clothing with power. It was granted as an abiding gift on Pentecost. It needs perpetual renewal. We may all have it. Without it, eloquence, learning, and all else, are but as sounding brass and a tinkling cymbal."[51]

The prophet, anointed with the Spirit, cannot avoid communicating what he feels about the gospel as well as what he thinks about it. The preacher must be involved emotionally as well as intellectually in what he proclaims. As one minister said to a group of his fellows, "Either put more fire into your sermons—or vice versa!"[52]

There is, of course, a profound difference between emotion and emotionalism. Emotionalism is the cheapening and exploitation of emotion. Yet Bartlett is right when he says, "Simply because emotion can become false, contrived, and artificial does not mean that we can deny that deep feeling is a part of great preaching. When it is used for its own sake, emotion becomes cheap and unhealthy. But when it comes as a sincere response to the meaning of the gospel, it is cleansing and lifting and a power for good."[53]

Richard Baxter may speak for us all when he says in his classic little volume on the pastoral ministry entitled *The Reformed Pastor,* "I marvel how I can preach . . . slightly and coldly, how I can let men alone in their sins and that I do not go to them and beseech them for

[51]Alexander Maclaren; quoted by Whitesell, *op. cit.,* p. 142.

[52]Charles E. Moser, "Portrait of a Minister," *Pulpit Digest,* June, 1962.

[53]*Op. cit.,* p. 54.

the Lord's sake to repent, however they may take it and whatever pains or trouble it should cost me. I seldom come out of the pulpit but my conscience smiteth me that I have been no more serious and fervent. It accuseth me not so much for want of human ornaments or elegance, nor for letting fall an uncomely word; but it asketh me: 'How could'st thou speak of life and death with such a heart? Should'st thou not weep over such a people, and should not thy tears interrupt thy words? Should'st not thou cry aloud and shew them their transgressions and entreat and beseech them as for life and death?' "[54]

VI

The next word of importance in describing the oral communication of divine truth by the minister is *parakalein,* to exhort, entreat, beseech, or admonish. The noun that describes the exhortation or entreaty is *paraklesis.* Its etymological meaning is the act of summoning a helper, from *para,* "to the side," and *kaleo,* "I call." The one who is thus called alongside is the *parakletos,* the title Jesus applied to the Holy Spirit in the Last Supper discourses of John's Gospel, and which John applies to Christ in I John 2:2.

To prevent an already long study from going completely out of bounds, we may let exhortation stand for a whole group of what Grady Davis calls "therapeutic" terms for preaching—those designed for the changing and improving of the believer.[55] Included in this group are words for encouragement or consolation (*paramutheomai*), to put in mind or admonish (*nouthetein*),

[54]Quoted by Stott, *op. cit.,* p. 58.

[55]*Op. cit.,* pp. 127-32.

to strengthen or confirm (*episterizein*), to build up or edify (*oikodomeo*), to rebuke, expose, convict (*elegchein, epitiman,* and *epiplessein*), and to discuss, dispute, argue (*dialegomai*).

Common to all these, and most nearly subsumed under exhortation, is the idea of challenge. Exhortation is "a knock on the door," a "note of summons." It is, as we have seen in connection with New Testament prophecy, one of the three functions of prophetic preaching: "He that prophesieth speaketh unto men to edification, and exhortation, and comfort" (I Cor. 14:3). It is essentially a demand for decision.

Here is one of the chief differences between preaching and lecturing or editorializing. Preaching demands response. Henry Ward Beecher said, "A sermon is not like a Chinese fire-cracker to be fired off for the noise which it makes. It is the hunter's gun, and at every discharge he should look to see his game fall."[56] Roy Pearson wrote, "Good preaching is always for a verdict. 'Answer!' it demands of its congregation. 'Answer "Yes" or answer "No," but before you turn away and go back to your common tasks, answer!'" And Mr. Pearson adds, "If preaching changes nothing, it accomplishes nothing."[57]

Whatever one may think of the whole of Rudolph Bultmann's theology, there is little room to quarrel with his definition of preaching: "What do we mean by *preaching*? Obviously, preaching is not the simple communication of facts. The reporting of a discovery made by scientific or historical research is not preaching. Likewise, preaching must be distinguished from teaching or

[56]Quoted by James S. Stewart, *Heralds of God* (New York: Charles Scribner's Sons, 1946), p. 121.

[57]*Op. cit.*, p. 24.

instruction: the presentation of mathematical or philosophical subjects, for example, is not preaching. Why not? Because preaching means a declaration which speaks directly to the hearer and challenges him to a specific reaction."[58]

This fact about preaching is what constitutes it, in Alan Richardson's words, a matter of self-judgment. Richardson wrote, "Not only in the spectacular events of world history . . . is the judgment of God now being manifested. It is a process that is going on wherever the word of God is being proclaimed; men are judging themselves, as it were, according to their acceptance or rejection of the Gospel (Heb. 4:12f.). Evil-doers will hate the light, and they are judged already (John 3:18-20); to reject the preaching of Christ's name is to reject *zoe* (life), which is the same thing as to incur the wrath of God (John 3:36). By our acceptance of Christ in this day of opportunity we anticipate the verdict of 'the last day' (John 3:18; 12:48)."[59]

This is not to be construed to mean that the response to exhortation must be visible to be real. The response may take various forms. Clifford defines preaching as "the proclamation of the word of God, in which the Lord Himself confronts the believing congregation in saving and sanctifying grace, calling forth adoration, thanksgiving, repentance, and self-oblation."[60]

There is a sense in which the Word of God effects responses of which the hearer may not be at the moment

[58]*Religion and Culture,* p. 236; quoted by Howard Williams, *Down to Earth* (Naperville, Ill.: SCM Book Club, 1946), p. 76.

[59]*An Introduction to the Theology of the New Testament* (New York: Harper and Brothers, 1959), p. 78.

[60]*Op. cit.,* p. 50.

aware. Both Oswald Chambers and Gene Bartlett have noted this. Chambers wrote, "We may see no result in our congregation, but if we have presented the truth and anyone has seen it for one second, he can never be the same again, a new element has come into his life. It is essential to remember this and not to estimate the success of preaching by immediate results."[61] And Bartlett adds, "The deeper reality is that preaching actually brings new qualities of life to those who share in the experience. It is not an idea about the Christian life; it is life itself which is given. In a profound way the real experience is one of personal fulfillment and re-creation. When preaching is at its highest a man comes away from it saying not simply 'I ought,' though there are great ethical imperatives, not 'I will,' though there are great decisions. Deeper than these, he comes away saying 'I am'; for to some degree, or in some aspect, he is a new creation. Something has happened in him and to him. The mark of the preaching is not something he has heard, but something he has become. It is not a new definition he has received, but a new dimension of life itself."[62]

Preaching, to conform to the meaning of exhortation, must make a difference. Every sermon should seek wider understandings, broader insights, yielded and changed lives, and cleansed hearts. The seminarian who brought his sermon to the homiletics instructor with the question, "Will my sermon do?" received the only appropriate answer: "Do what?" Roy L. Smith tells of a young man from India who visited a number of American churches. He said, "I was greatly impressed by the

[61]*The Moral Foundations of Life* (London: Marshall, Morgan and Scott, Ltd., 1962), p. 20.

[62]*Op. cit.*, p. 47.

fact that the pews were all cushioned. There seemed even to be cushions in the sermons."[63]

But I would not leave this group of terms revolving around the idea of exhortation without calling attention to one very important aspect of their total meaning. This is the inclusion of the idea of consolation or comfort. "Exhortation, and comfort" are conjoined in the twice-quoted verse from I Corinthians (14:3). The *Parakletos,* in addition to being called the Counsellor, the Advocate, the Helper, is also called the Comforter.

John Henry Jowett years ago called attention to this function of preaching: "I have been greatly impressed in recent years," he wrote, "by one refrain which I have found running through many biographies. Dr. Parker repeated again and again, 'Preach to broken hearts!' And here is the testimony of Ian Maclaren: 'The chief end of preaching is comfort. . . .' Never can I forget what a distinguished scholar, who used to sit in my church, once said to me: 'Your best work in the pulpit has been to put heart into men for the coming week!' And may I bring you an almost bleeding passage from Dr. Dale: 'People want to be comforted. . . . They need consolation —really need it, and do not merely long for it.' "[64]

More recently, William Barclay has said, "So then preaching should equip and educate the mind; preaching should challenge and kindle the will. But there is still another part of man. *Preaching must speak to the heart.* No man will ever be a preacher unless he bears his people on his heart. The one thing that the preacher

[63]The author has been unable to find the exact page in *The Future Is upon Us* (New York: Abingdon Press, 1962).

[64]*The Preacher, His Life and Work,* p. 107; quoted, Stott, *op. cit.,* p. 91.

must never forget is the human need of the people before him."[65]

VII

The final term for preaching we shall consider is one that comes very close to home. To preach is to witness—*martyrein.* Paul relates his commission from Christ as constituting him "a minister and a witness" (Acts 26:16). This is also peculiarly John's word for preaching. He uses hardly any other.

That the minister is a witness says two things. It reminds us that true preaching is costly. Witness is the word from which *martyr* is derived. The witness, as the martyr, stakes the whole of his life on the reality of the gospel.

Bishop J. Paul Taylor vividly illustrates this with an anecdote: "Atop the roof of a building on a theological seminary campus is a large stone figure of a pelican surrounded by her fledglings. I heard a former professor in the seminary tell of going to the campus one day before the stone figure was lifted to its place on the ridge of the roof, and observing a negro employee of the school looking intently at it, he drew near. Whereupon the man asked the professor what the figure meant. He related the fable of the pelican tearing her breast open with her beak to feed her starving little ones on her life blood, when no food could be found. The negro was solemnly silent for a few moments, and then replied, 'I hopes and prays that this bird will build her nest in the heart of every preacher boy who come here to study.' "

Bishop Taylor continues, "Certainly the heart's blood, as well as sweat and tears, must be put into our

[65]*Fishers of Men,* p. 109.

service if a dying world is to be saved. . . . Witness is a word with blood in it, for there is love in it, and love bleeds. It is the only way we can bless the world. The word bless meant originally 'to consecrate with blood,' so the words blood and bless are closely related."[66]

It will always be true that preaching which costs nothing accomplishes nothing.

That the minister is a witness also derives meaning from the modern use of the term witness. To witness is to speak from personal experience. Hearsay evidence will not be accepted, either in court or in the pulpit. Albeit used here in an adapted sense, "The husbandman must be first partaker of the fruits." This is both his privilege and his obligation. The preacher can no more truly preach what he has not experienced than he can come back from where he has never been. "Right well hast thou described this coin," is the hearer's response to the preacher; "but tell me, dost thou have it in thy pocket?"

The sermon is the lengthened shadow of the man.[67] Without the vitality of personal experience, Christian preaching would have been crushed by persecution within six weeks. The searching question addressed by Jesus to Pilate is always appropriate to the preacher, "Sayest thou this of thyself, or did others tell it thee concerning me?" (John 18:34) "Preaching is speaking truth whose vital and eternal significance has been seen, whose force has been felt and grasped in one's own spirit."[68]

Bishop Ralph Cushman tells of a godly layman in an eastern city who put his hands on the preacher's

[66]*Op. cit.,* pp. 116-17.

[67]Earl H. Furguson in Wayne Oates, *op. cit.,* p. 130.

[68]Weatherspoon, *op. cit.,* p. 58.

shoulders one day and rather yearningly said, "I wish you ministers would sometimes stand up in your pulpits, and throwing away your manuscripts, would just stand there and tell us what God in Christ means to you."[69]

Daniel T. Niles has offered an unforgettable illustration of what it means for the preacher to be a witness. He points out that witnessing is of three kinds. One may witness as a spectator, as one involved, or as one deeply and personally affected. For example, an automobile accident may be witnessed in three ways: by a spectator standing on the street corner; by a passenger in one of the cars; or by one who has been injured in and his life directly affected by the accident. The context of preaching is that something has happened to the preacher himself. He must be part of the evidence that his message is true. Preaching catches fire from the sparks that fly from the anvil of our own experience as God hammers us out according to His will and purpose. The word that judges others must first judge us.[70]

Ian M. Fraser defined preaching as "essentially the summoning of men to hear with the preacher and through his words God's living Word, the summoning of men to stand, alert, under an Authority to whom the preacher testifies and submits."[71]

It is, of course, as Peter Forsyth said, not the fact of our experience but the fact which we experience on which we stand.[72] We are witnesses, not to ourselves,

[69]*The Essentials of Evangelism* (Nashville: General Board of Evangelism, The Methodist Church, 1946), p. 67.

[70]*Op. cit.*, pp. 104-5.

[71]*Scottish Journal of Theology,* XII, No. 3 (September, 1959), 329.

[72]*The Principle of Authority,* p. 178; quoted by Donald Macleod, "The Creative Preacher," *Bulletin of Crozer Theological Seminary,* April, 1962, p. 5.

but to our Saviour. Clifford reminds us of the practice of Michelangelo in working with a candle strapped to his forehead lest his shadow fall across the marble he was sculpturing.[73] We must avoid casting the shadow of our own notions and idiosyncrasies across the face of the Master we seek to commend.

What shall we say then to these things? Just that preaching is telling forth the good news of salvation as a herald proclaims the message of his king, teaching the Word with the anointing of the Spirit, exhorting our hearers to follow us as we follow Christ.

As Milo Arnold cautions, "The man in the small church needs to remember that there is no small gospel, no small Christian ministry, and no small pulpit. There may be small groups of people who need his ministry and there may be small communities which need pastors, but there is no excuse for small sermons or small preachers. The people of the smallest parish need just as big sermons and as lofty services as the people in the largest congregation. They have a right to expect a man's very best under God. No man can afford to give less than his best to any service; for the moment he does, he lowers his best to something beneath what it might be."[73]

"Privilege carries responsibility," wrote James W. Clarke. "Responsibility prophesies judgment. May we never forget that there will come a day when we shall stand before the great white throne, and from its midst there shall sound a voice like unto that of the Son of God, asking, 'I gave you my gospel, what did you do with it?' "[74]

[73]*Op. cit.*, p. 75.

[74]*Dynamic Preaching* (Westwood, N.J.: Fleming H. Revell, 1960), p. 46.

Oft when the Word is on me to deliver
Lifts the illusion and the truth lies bare;
Desert or throng, the city or the river,
Melts in a lucid paradise of air—

Only like souls I see the folk thereunder,
Bound who should conquer, slaves who should be kings—
Hearing their one hope with an empty wonder,
Sadly contented in a show of things.

Then with a rush the intolerable craving
Shivers through me like a trumpet call—
Oh, to save these, to perish for their saving,
Die for their life, be offered for them all!

—From F. W. H. Myers, "St. Paul"

CHAPTER 5

The Minister as Pastor

The pastoral function in the modern ministry is best represented in the biblical metaphor of shepherd. The idea of the religious leader as a shepherd is common to both the Old Testament and the New.

In the Old Testament, it is mainly the unfaithful shepherd who is in view—the unfaithful priest or the false prophet. "His watchmen are blind: they are all ignorant, they are all dumb dogs, they cannot bark; sleeping, lying down, loving to slumber. Yea, they are greedy dogs which can never have enough, and they are shepherds that cannot understand: they all look to his own way, every one for his gain, from his quarter" (Isa. 56:10-11).

"The pastors are become brutish, and have not sought the Lord: therefore they shall not prosper, and all their flocks shall be scattered" (Jer. 10:21). "Woe be unto the pastors that destroy and scatter the sheep of my pasture! saith the Lord" (Jer. 23:1). "My people hath been lost sheep: their shepherds have caused them to go astray, they have turned them away on the mountains: they have gone from mountain to hill, they have forgotten their restingplace" (Jer. 50:6).

Ezekiel delivered a memorable oracle against the unfaithful shepherds of Israel in Ezek. 34:1-31. Prophetic of Christ's use of the term, he cites the promise: "And I will set one shepherd over them, and he shall feed them, even my servant David; he shall feed them, and he shall be their shepherd" (Ezek. 34:23). The Messianic age will see the office of shepherd entrusted to faithful men: "And I will set up shepherds over them which shall feed them: and they shall fear no more, nor be dismayed, neither shall they be lacking, saith the Lord" (Jer. 23:4). "I will give you pastors according to mine heart, which shall feed you with knowledge and understanding" (Jer. 3:15).

In the New Testament, as we have earlier seen, Christ is the Good Shepherd (John 10:11, 14), and the specter of the faithless shepherd still appears as the hireling who leaves the sheep when the wolf comes (John 10:12). Yet the promise of the true shepherd is fulfilled in the relation of the elders or overseers of the church to "the flock" (Acts 20:17, 28) and in the listing of the pastoral function as one of the offices of the New Testament ministry in Eph. 4:11.

While I Pet. 5:1-4 does not employ the term shepherd or pastor specifically, save in relation to the Chief Shepherd, the pastoral function is clearly described: "The elders which are among you I exhort, who am also an elder, and a witness of the sufferings of Christ, and also a partaker of the glory that shall be revealed: Feed the flock of God which is among you, taking the oversight thereof, not by constraint, but willingly; not for filthy lucre, but of a ready mind; neither as being lords over God's heritage, but being ensamples to the flock. And when the chief Shepherd shall appear, ye shall receive a crown of glory that fadeth not away."

The pastoral office is implied if not stated in the

more frequent references to actual or potential followers of Christ as sheep. False prophets, though ravening wolves, come in sheep's clothing (Matt. 7:15). The multitudes were as sheep having no shepherd (Matt. 9:36; Mark 6:34). The people of Israel were as lost sheep (Matt. 10:6). The company of the finally redeemed are the sheep as contrasted with the goats (Matt. 25:33). Christ seeks His other sheep, not of this fold (John 10:16). Peter's mission is to feed the lambs and the sheep (John 21:15-17). As sheep that had gone astray, we have now returned unto the Shepherd and Bishop of our souls (I Pet. 2:25).

It may readily be admitted that the comparison of people with sheep should not be pushed too far. It may also be recognized that the ministry of today differs more greatly from that of New Testament times in its functions of pastoring and overseeing than it does in its work of preaching. It is still important to recognize the distinctive challenge of the pastoral phase of a New Testament ministry in our day.

I

There is a sense, of course, in which any division of the functions of a total ministry is somewhat artificial. The minister is a whole man interacting with the whole needs of whole persons. To draw sharp lines between preparing, preaching, pastoring, and administration is not as simple as it seems at first. The same leader serves the same people in all these ways, and what he is and does in one capacity carries across into all the others.

Seward Hiltner in *The Christian Shepherd* divides the minister's functions into three categories—shepherding, communicating, and organizing. "Each under proper circumstances," he says, "becomes the principal concern. . . . Shepherding . . . does not describe the total function of the person we call a 'pastor.' He is also one who communicates the gospel and organizes the followship."[1]

The close and essential relationship between effective preaching and the whole of the pastoral ministry is almost too obvious to be missed. Phillips Brooks said, "The preacher who is not a pastor grows remote. The pastor who is not a preacher grows petty. . . . Be both; for you cannot really be one unless you are also the other."[2] Clifford claims that "the key to effective preaching lies in a genuine pastoral ministry."[3]

Charles F. Kemp in his work on *Pastoral Preaching* points out two apparently contrasting but actually complementary statements by Charles E. Jefferson, pastor of Broadway Tabernacle in New York many years ago. In 1904, Jefferson wrote: "The work of preaching is the most difficult of all the things which a minister is called to do. Indeed, it is the most difficult task to which any mortal can set himself. It is at once the most strenuous and the most exacting of all forms of labor. It requires a fuller combination of faculties and a finer balance of powers than are required in any other department of human effort."

Eight years later, Jefferson published a volume on *The Minister as Shepherd*. In this he wrote, "It is a work which requires extraordinary wisdom, unfailing patience, plodding fidelity, unfaltering boldness, a genius for hope, abiding faith, and boundless love, but there

[1]Quoted by Charles F. Kemp, *Pastoral Preaching* (St. Louis, Mo.: The Bethany Press, 1963), pp. 20-21.

[2]Quoted by Clifford, *op. cit.*, p. 65.

[3]*Ibid.*, p. 64.

is none other that is more clearly the work that Christ just now wishes done, and upon the faithful performance of which the future of humanity more manifestly depends. The cities must be saved, and they are to be saved by shepherds."[4] Again, there is no contradiction. The minister must be both preacher and shepherd.

Harry Emerson Fosdick told a group of ministerial students to whom he was lecturing that their chief problem would be learning to understand the people they would be called to serve. He said, "It is to be assumed that you will know the gospel and that you will understand the subjects on which you preach; but will you understand what is happening in and to the lives of those to whom you preach? Preaching is wrestling with individuals over questions of life and death, and until that idea of it commands a preacher's mind and method, eloquence will avail him little and theology not at all."[5]

There are various ways in which the total pastoral function may be analyzed. Some would view it as including everything which does not specifically fall under the head of public oral communication of the gospel. Thus Kent cites five main functions belonging to the pastoral ministry:

1. The pastoral—shepherding the flock of God, feeding and caring for its members (Acts 20:28; I Pet. 4:2).

2. The educational—teaching the church (I Tim. 3:2; 5:17).

3. The officiative—leading in the worship and activities of the church (Jas. 5:14).

[4]*Op. cit.*, p. 17.

[5]Quoted, George K. Bowers, *op. cit.*, pp. 105-6.

4. The representative—officially representing the church at certain times (Acts 20:17).

5. The administrative—ruling in the church, not as a dictator, but by precept and example (I Tim. 5:7; I Pet. 5:2-3).[6]

It is, of course, more specifically with the shepherding function that we are here concerned. At risk of oversimplification, this might be divided into three areas: caring, calling, and counselling.

II

Daniel Day Williams has argued for the use of the phrase "the care of souls" in place of the more venerable "cure of souls." There is something to be said for this altered terminology, "because we can always care even when we cannot cure."[7]

Whatever else caring means—and it means much—the ministry of the shepherd heart must be person-centered. Never will people be thought of as statistics, units to be counted. They are, however deformed by sin and unlovely to the natural eye, precious souls who have been bought with a price beyond compare. Until our love for people approximates that of our Saviour, we are far more apt to be hirelings than genuine under-shepherds.

Pastoral care involves many concerns. Augustine has left us a classic statement: "Disturbers are to be rebuked, the low-spirited are to be encouraged, the in-

[6]Homer A. Kent, Sr., *The Pastor and His Work* (Chicago: The Moody Press, 1963), p. 211.

[7]*The Minister and the Care of Souls* (New York: Harper and Brothers, 1961), p. 9.

firm to be supported, objectors confuted, the treacherous guarded against, the unskilled taught, the lazy aroused, the contentious restrained, the haughty repressed, litigants pacified, the poor relieved, the oppressed liberated, the good approved, the evil borne with, and all are to be loved."[8]

Martin Bucer (d. 1551) gives us a fivefold analysis that adds an important note: "To draw to Christ those who are alienated; to lead back those who have been drawn away; to secure amendment of life in those who fall into sin; to strengthen weak and sickly Christians; to preserve Christians who are whole and strong, and urge them forward in all good."[9] Here we have the need for conservation, for maintaining and strengthening the spiritual life induced through evangelism.

There is more than just a little evidence to show that conserving the results of soul winning is not one of the strongest points of evangelistic churches. While we are bringing new people in through the front door, too many are slipping out the back door because somewhere along the line we fail at the task of conservation.

This is by no means a plea for less in the way of evangelism. Yet there is little permanent value in raising chickens for the hawks. If we espoused a theology which teaches that a single moment of faith and one act of receiving Christ insure final and eternal salvation, there would be some understanding of an attitude which regards the altar as an end in itself. But we do not accept such an understanding of Scripture. We affirm the need for perseverance in the faith with all it requires by way

[8]Quoted by Frederic Greeves, *Theology and the Cure of Souls* (Manhasset, N.Y.: Channel Press, Inc., 1962), p. 10.

[9]*Ibid.*, p. 11.

of nurture and pastoral care. We need therefore the more diligently to "strengthen weak and sickly Christians" and "to preserve Christians who are whole and strong, and urge them forward in all good."

III

Calling is a second function of the shepherd in our day. The need for it has not diminished with the changing emphases of pastoral work. There are still the widows and fatherless to be visited in their affliction (Jas. 1:27), a visitation ministry to the sick (Matt. 25:36) and to those imprisoned by circumstances as well as by steel bars.

Bishop Henry Knox Sherrill wrote in his autobiography:

> I am told that times have changed and what with the modern tempo of life and the new housing conditions, this home visitation is impractical. I do not believe it for a moment. It is a rationalization of the unwillingness of many to undertake an apparently pedestrian task. I realize that there is a great pressure upon the clergyman of today to have the institution of the parish move forward in all of its organizations and activities. However, in the past twenty years I have travelled throughout the breadth of our church and everywhere I have heard the same complaint from the laity that they do not see their clergymen in their homes. It apparently makes no difference whether the parish is large or small. If I were to suggest a means of spiritual revival in the Church, it would not be the creation of new organizations or slogans, but having every minister call every day, resolutely and persistently. I belong to an older generation, but it strikes me that many ministers are too concerned with themselves. Perhaps there is an excessive introspection encouraged in our seminaries. To find his life, the best thing any minister can do is to lose it in the lives of his people. This is not done

by uttering broad generalities about sheep, but by knowing well each of his own flock."[10]

A limited part of the function of pastoral calling may be accomplished through formalized counselling programs and procedures. There is need for caution at this point, however. Bishop Leslie Ray Marston underlines it:

> Nor should the minister, who sets certain hours of his day for counseling in his office or study, mistakenly conclude that thereby he has discharged his responsibilities in pastoral visitation. Although each complements the other, pastoral counseling and pastoral visitation are not the same. A first principle of counseling holds that the counselee seek the counselor, but those who most need pastoral help often are those who will seek to avoid the pastor in face-to-face encounter. The shepherd must search out his foot-sore, bruised, and wandering sheep where they are.[11]

Charles F. Kemp makes the same point:

> Sometimes, however, a pastor may have a parishioner who needs help but does not seek it—what then? The pastor has an advantage over other professions . . . he can call with no embarrassment, with no need for an explanation. Through a call he can make himself available. Sometimes this is all that is needed. Many a person has opened up and stated a problem simply because the pastor called when this same person would never have gone to the pastor's study to seek his help.
>
> Sometimes the person won't, however; then the pastor may need to risk his relationship for the person's own good. He states frankly but understandingly his reasons for being there. "It has come to my attention that . . . I wonder if there is anything I can do to help?" Much depends on "how" the pastor makes such a contact.

[10]*Among Friends: An Autobiography;* quoted by James Kennedy, *op. cit.*, pp. 162-63.

[11]Kenneth Geiger, compiler, *Further Insights into Holiness* (Kansas City, Mo.: Beacon Hill Press, 1963), p. 309.

> There must be no appearance of prying or of condemnation. It must be a sincere desire to help.[12]

Clifford lists the objectives of pastoral calling, which, he says, has a purpose as definite and inherent as the visit of a doctor or a social worker:

1. To get to know the people behind their Sunday dress-up.

2. To build a relationship in which he can mediate the presence of Christ himself in the crises of their lives in a way that no stranger can.

3. To widen the horizons of those he goes to see.

4. To prepare the ground and open the way for counseling.[13]

Each of these points is significant. Two of them especially demand an additional comment.

The shepherd knows and is known by his sheep (John 10:14). The only way this can be on any more than a casual basis is that he shall do as Ezekiel did when he reported, "I sat where they sat" (Ezek. 3:15). Only by such contacts can the pastor know the real problems of his people. The late W. E. Sangster wrote, "Speaking broadly, his task on Sunday is to answer, with all the richness of theological and Biblical scholarship that he can command, the questions his people have been asking him—perhaps unconsciously—during the week."[14]

[12]"On the Work of the Pastor," the *Christian,* Vol. C, No. 47 (November 25, 1962), 15.

[13]*Op. cit.*, pp. 73-80.

[14]*The Approach to Preaching* (Philadelphia: The Westminster Press, 1953), p. 80.

IV

The last point in Clifford's summary leads to a consideration of the place of counseling in the pastor's work. For all the changes that have taken place in our understanding of human motivation and needs, counseling is basically as old as man-to-man relationships. Behind the changing terminology are the same situations in which experience helps inexperience, wisdom aids folly, and the strong support the weak.

In the Old Testament, counsel was primarily the mood of the wise man, who along with prophet and priest communicated the truth from one generation and one level of maturity and understanding to another. The Son upon whose shoulder would rest the government was to be called Counsellor, or probably more exactly, Wonderful Counsellor (Isa. 9:6). One of the translations of the Greek term for the Holy Spirit in John's Gospel is "Counselor," with all the varied richness the English term connotes.[15] In the Corinthian correspondence we are permitted to "listen in" while a master counselor answers questions in what we could hardly describe as a nondirective fashion.

This is not the time nor the place, nor have I the ability, to give a technical discussion of the vast and growing field of counseling. I can but indicate some of the basic considerations in the exercise of this phase of the minister's role as shepherd.

[15]"The New Testament teaching with reference to the Holy Spirit is indispensable wisdom for the practice of pastoral counseling. Especially relevant is the Revised Standard translation of the name of the Paraclete as 'the Counselor.' This translation of the name is certainly the proper description of the character of God as seen in both the Old and New Testaments."—Wayne C. Oates, *Protestant Pastoral Counseling* (Philadelphia: The Westminster Press, 1962), p. 57.

It is particularly important that we recognize the distinctiveness of pastoral counseling. Pastoral counseling must never be confused with psychological counselling, occupational or educational counseling, or even marriage counseling as such—although the pastor may find occasion to do some of all kinds of counseling. Pastoral counseling is thoroughly distinctive in two basic ways: first, as to its objective; and second, as to the role of the pastor as counselor.

Clifford has listed the purposes of pastoral counselling as (1) to enable a person to arrive at better understanding of himself and the nature of his problems; (2) To help the counselee to achieve integration of personality around a worthy spiritual ideal; and (3), its primary objective, to effect the reconciliation of man to God. Clifford further notes that the pastor "has to find a way of combining the permissive attitude, whereby a person is encouraged to exercise his priesthood to the limits of his capacity, with the role of spiritual director, commissioned to mediate the whole counsel of God." And again he says, "One thing is certain: the pastoral office is unique as far as method is concerned. General counseling techniques are to be welcomed and used as far as they are applicable; but they cannot be taken over without modification: they have to be interwoven with the ultimate purpose of the Christian Church—the reconciliation of man to God through Christ."[16]

Along with consideration of more incidental matters, the distinctive role of the pastor as counselor is stressed by Wayne Oates in *Protestant Pastoral Counseling.* Dr. Oates finds four basic elements prerequisite to effective counseling. (1) The person in need must want to meet

[16]*Op. cit.,* pp. 83-87, 115-16.

with the pastor enough to take a measure of initiative on his own. (2) The pastor should have a reasonably private, adequate, and uncompromisingly appropriate place for his counseling. (3) The pastor should control and determine the time factor himself, and not leave this entirely with the counselee. (4) The pastor's role must be clearly defined and mutually understood.[17] One of the distinctive elements in the pastor's role, Oates says, is his reliance "upon the realities of spiritual conception and maturation within the life of man through the creative activity of the Holy Spirit."[18]

Dr. Oates also cautions the pastor against overlooking the resources of the Christian community in his counseling. The church itself contributes to the support and guidance of its members. "Many of the people in a pastor's community," he notes, "are already depending upon each other for emotional aid and guidance. The pastor does not need to perceive himself as just a 'counselor' to whom everyone must come. He cuts off the resources of the natural forces of helpfulness within a community itself should he insist on being *the* counselor. However, if he perceives himself as the pastoral guide of a purposeful fellowship of people who have a creative and redemptive intention toward each other, he can mobilize the resources of the whole community in both the prevention and the cure of some highly personal problems."[19]

Furthermore, "the spiritually secure pastor knows that the life of his counselee is actually in the hands of God, and not his. The Holy Spirit and not he himself is the Counselor. The processes of purpose in this life

[17]*Op. cit.*, p. 169.

[18]*Ibid.*, p. 105.

[19]Quoted, Mullen, *op. cit.*, p. 98.

situation are deeper than his own power to probe. Consequently, he can 'rest himself in these thoughts.' He does not have to rush to defend God. He does not mistake his own insecurity for the precariousness of a flimsy god's position in the world. He can take people's troubles seriously without overdeveloped and overworked feelings of responsibility that keep him awake at night, worrying about all the problems people have presented to him the day before."[20]

The pastor's privilege and responsibility to take the initiative is another aspect of the distinctiveness of his master role as a man of God. This fact and the limitations inherent in it are both described by Oates:

> One of the hallmarks of the pastoral ministry is that we have the right to take initiative toward people, to go to them, and to express concern about them.
>
> However, we must respect the privacy and the individual freedom of a person in the process of taking initiative. Our objective should be to stimulate their own initiative in such a way that they will want help with whatever degree of initiative we take toward them. In other words, we are confusing our relationship to people when we take full responsibility for all the initiative, and relieve them of the health and strength that comes to them when they are stimulated to be wholesomely concerned about their own destinies. . . . A part of the great task of being an effective Protestant pastor is in knowing where the line of balance for the initiative between the counselor and the counselee lies.[21]

In all counseling, again, the role of the pastor "should be clearly and mutually understood. The person should understand clearly that the pastor is not just another *neighbor* peering into the situation, not just another *friend* trying to be nice and friendly, not just

[20]Oates, *op. cit.*, p. 59.
[21]*Ibid.*, pp. 153-54.

another *relative* with a vested interest and a 'side' in the matter, and not just a *preacher* looking for illustrations with which to dramatize his sermons. Rather, he is a *pastor* appointed by men and called by God to minister with confidence and commitment to all concerned."[22]

V

One of the most important contributions to the life of another the pastor makes in his counseling is in the assurance he gives of care and love for one in trouble. The normal reaction of a person in difficulty is a sense of isolation. His greatest need may be the simple awareness that he is not alone. Williams tells of a counselor who had rather unskillfully tried to help another through a serious crisis by saying that he was "sure the person would come through all right." Out of this came the most important lesson he had learned about therapy. When the crisis was past, his counselee told him, "What I most needed to know was not that I would come through all right, but that you and the others upon whom I depend would love me no matter what happened."[23]

It is this element of caring that distinguishes between true counseling and the rather casual giving of advice that can be done on the basis of a single brief contact. Oates contrasts this application of what may be pridefully called common sense to any and all problems, with the attitude of the counselor who "encourages the person, through the processes of spiritual maturity and insight, to lay hold of and to deal with

[22]*Ibid.*, p. 247.
[23]*Op. cit.*, p. 91.

his own problem." The pastor assures him that "he is not left alone. . . . [and] gives him spiritual fellowship and assistance in the pilgrimage of growth."[24]

Such caring is costly. The pastor must guard against the situation sketched in the pathos of the lines:

Last night, O friend of mine, unto your door
With wearied soul and heart most sore,
I came to cry for comfort. And you
Gave me light words, light praise, your jester's due:
I shall not come for comfort any more.

Take you my laughter, since you love it so.
The little jests men juggle to and fro.
I did not guess how much I came to ask,
I did not guess how difficult the task
Your solace for a heart you did not know.[25]

It is never really appropriate to contrast the varied segments of a pastor's work. None of them can be neglected or relegated to a minor position without distortion and damage to the image of the whole. The man of God must be a whole man, entire and complete in both personal life and public ministry. The disciple and the herald must also be the shepherd. It is said that among the reasons given by Theodore Roosevelt for attending church was his comment that, whatever the quality of the sermon one may hear, "he will hear a sermon by a good man who, with his good wife, is engaged all the week in making hard lives a little easier."

[24] *Op. cit.*, p. 107.

[25] Author unknown; quoted by Alexander Stewart, *The Shock of Revelation* (New York: The Seabury Press, 1967), p. 144.

And that, when you come right down to it, is worth everything.

Grace Noll Crowell has penned lines she calls "A Pastor to His People."

You are my people, given me to love,
To serve, to shepherd through the days ahead:
I pray God that I may be worthy of
This honor; I am glad that I was led
To come to you, that through God's gentle grace
My lines have fallen in this pleasant place.

I would be strong to work where there is need;
I would be true to serve you as I should;
And I would give the Bread of Life to feed
Each hungry soul who comes to me for food;
And I would honor with my every word
The blessed Saviour—Jesus Christ, our Lord.

I plead with you for patience. Should I make
An error, I would gladly make amends,
Or if some unintentional mistake
Be mine, I need your understanding, friends.
As pastor and as people, may we be
Builders together, for eternity!

CHAPTER 6

The Minister as Overseer

We look now at a function of the ministry best described by the New Testament term *episkopos,* overseer or bishop, and its parallel *presbyteros,* or elder. In the account of Paul's contact with the leaders of the church at Ephesus in Acts 20, the elders of the church (v. 17) are called overseers of the flock (v. 28). The same identification is made in Titus 1:5 and 7.

The overseer is literally "the one who looks or watches over." The English term bishop originally had almost precisely the same meaning, although now it has come to designate an ecclesiastical official who has responsibility for the work of other ministers. *Presbyteros* is a comparative form of *presbus,* an old man or elder. It is used both of seniority in age and of rank or position. W. E. Vine distinguishes between the two titles: "The term 'elder' indicates the mature spiritual experience and understanding of those so described; the term 'bishop,' or 'overseer,' indicates the character of the work undertaken."[1]

[1] *Op. cit.,* I, 128-29.

It is quite obvious that most of what would today be included within the administrative tasks of the minister was quite unknown in Bible times. There is, however, the record of Jethro's wise advice to Moses when the great lawgiver's father-in-law saw how encumbered Moses was with details: "The thing that thou doest is not good. Thou wilt surely wear away, both thou, and this people that is with thee: for this thing is too heavy for thee; thou art not able to perform it thyself alone. Hearken now unto my voice, I will give thee counsel, and God shall be with thee: Be thou for the people to God-ward, that thou mayest bring the causes unto God: and thou shalt teach them ordinances and laws, and shalt shew them the way wherein they must walk, and the work that they must do. Moreover thou shalt provide out of all the people able men, such as fear God, men of truth, hating covetousness; and place such over them, to be rulers of thousands, and rulers of hundreds, rulers of fifties, and rulers of tens: and let them judge the people at all seasons: and it shall be, that every great matter they shall bring unto thee, but every small matter they shall judge: so shall it be easier for thyself, and they shall bear the burden with thee" (Exod. 18:17-22).

Similarly, there is the account in Acts 6:2-4 of the action taken when the demands of a growing church began to cut in on the time and strength of the apostles. Calling the church together, the Twelve said, "It is not right that we should give up preaching the word of God to serve tables. Therefore, brethren, pick out from among you seven men of good repute, full of the Spirit and of wisdom, whom we may appoint to this duty. But we will devote ourselves to prayer and to the ministry of the word" (RSV).

These two examples were in themselves administrative arrangements, and indicate both the value and the necessity of administrative oversight. Yet the organizational machinery of the congregation of Israel and of early Christianity was a far cry from that which seems essential in these times. Someone has remarked that God calls a man to preach, but it seems as if the church calls him to do everything else but. Joseph Sittler in *The Ecology of Faith* remarks that "a minister has been ordained to an Office; he too often ends up running an office."[2]

Not many are as fortunate as the preacher who was met by the head of the official board when he went to a new pastorate and told that there were just two things his people wanted to say to him: "First, we want you to be a good example to the people in our church, and that means you won't be out every night of the week, away from home. And second, we don't want you to do anything in the church here that we can do."[3]

I

With all its more modern forms, the administrative responsibility incumbent on the minister is not entirely new. Paul, it has been said, "was just as concerned about expressing his pastoral ministry through raising money for the destitute people of Jerusalem as he was in helping a runaway slave with his problem with authority persons!"[4] And Jean Frederic Oberlin, who

[2](Philadelphia: Muhlenberg Press, 1961), p. 84.

[3]Reported by Joseph T. Bayly concerning Dr. Harold England, pastor of the Reformed church in Midland, Mich., in the *Advent Christian Witness*, May, 1962, p. 4.

[4]Oates, *op. cit.*, p. 124.

served a tiny village parish at Waldsbach in what was called the "Valley of Stone," wrote: "The pastor at Waldsbach, if he tries to be what he ought to be . . . is a poor dog, a beast of burden, and a cart horse. He must do everything, watch everything, provide for everything, answer for everything. From early morning until bedtime I am occupied, hurried, crushed without being able to do one-half or one-tenth part of what ought to be done. Everything rests upon the pastor."[5]

Byron LeJeune tells the story of a pastor in a smaller town who frequently disappeared for an hour at a time without leaving word with his wife or anyone else where he was going. The lady of the parsonage, though curious, hesitated to ask. Later she became alarmed. When she confided in an evangelist who came to the church, the evangelist said, "I'll follow him and see where he goes."

The pastor started out one afternoon with the evangelist trailing him. He climbed a little hill to a clearing, and sat down on a log overlooking the town below. Discovering the evangelist following, the pastor called, "Come up here. I want you to see something."

They sat down on the log together looking down at the village below. Nothing happened, except that a train came in, stopped at the station for a few minutes, and steamed out. The pastor said, "Did you see that?"

"See what?" his friend replied. "I only saw a train go through."

"That's just it," said the enthused pastor. "I have to get away every once in a while and come up here to watch that train. It's the only thing in this place that moves without my having to get behind it and push!"

[5]Quoted by Bartlett, *op. cit.*, p. 62.

II

There is no question but that many pastors find tension within themselves in reconciling their roles as shepherds and as overseers. Thomas Hughart put it incisively: "Organization means manipulation and managing persons as parts of a machine, whereas the pastoral role requires the kind of personal consideration that encourages the discovery of newness in life, and the free choice of ways to give it expression."[6] Yet effective coordination of the activities of people demands organization. And organization requires administration.

Any possible grouping of persons in pursuit of common objectives must have structure. This is the difference between a crowd and a company. The establishment and maintenance of structure is part of the task of the overseer. Says Thomas Mullen, "The Protestant minister is not set free to be a busy-body. He is set free to get the Body busy."[7]

In the little volume of sermons entitled *Fresh Every Morning,* Bishop Gerald Kennedy describes three philosophies of the ministry. One minister went to a church and said in effect, I am here for you to serve me. And the church did just that. It was willing to exist to glorify its gifted pastor. Another man went to a church and said, I am here to serve you. The people were content to take him at his word, and he became their errand boy. A third pastor went to a church and said, Come, let us serve Christ together. He it was, the bishop says, who understood the true nature of the ministry—"He was there to call every member of that church to the common service of the Lord."[8]

[6]In Cunningham, *op. cit.,* p. 21.

[7]*Op. cit.,* p. 90.

[8](New York: Harper and Row, 1966), pp. 47-48.

The complexities of pastoral administration are not altogether a function of size. Smaller churches are often more demanding than larger ones. More falls to the pastor, simply because there do not seem to be the people able or willing to serve.

Always the wholeness of the ministry must be kept in mind. Paul wrote, "This one thing I do," when actually he was doing many things—preaching, writing letters, directing the labors of others, providing for the permanence and stability of the infant churches he established, grappling with perplexing problems, and even raising money. He speaks of "that which cometh upon me daily, the care of all the churches" (II Cor. 11:28). But his claim to singleness of purpose was justified because everything he did was "going in the same direction, serving the same end."[9] As Gene Bartlett writes:

> The answer to the minister's loss of identity in his ministry is not first of all elimination of activities, but integration. If a man can recover the sense that he is about his ministry wherever he is in touch with people, then this is not necessarily a confinement to a stereotype someone else has imposed; it may be the extension of *his* concept of the ministry into all the several responsibilities which fill his week. By the very nature of his relationship which admits him to the deeply personal places of other people's lives, he cannot be "just an administrator" or a "mere executive." In all these he is consistently a pastor working among the people of God and in this reality he finds the wholeness of his ministry.[10]

III

Administration is a sort of catchall term for everything that goes into the direction, management, or leadership of any sort of activity. It is the executive function.

[9]Bartlett, *op. cit.*, p. 76.

[10]*Loc. cit.*

Defined from the standpoint of group process, administration is "working with people to set goals, to build organizational relationships, to distribute responsibility, to conduct programs, and to evaluate accomplishments." The "real focus of administration" is "the relationship with and between people."[11]

One writer has listed five administrative responsibilities: (1) The determination and clarification of function; (2) The formulation of policies and procedures; (3) The delegation of authority; (4) The selection, supervision, and training of the staff, and (5) The mobilization and organization of all available resources to accomplish the ends and purposes of the organization.[12]

In the church, these are the tasks of the pastor. Regardless of the organization, the responsibility for the coordination and effective activity of the group ultimately falls back upon the man whom God and the church have called. His leadership or lack of it can make or break the entire program. Douglas Horton expressed it well when he said, "The older I grow, the more clearly I see that leadership is basic. Time and again we have witnessed in a church a change for the better or for worse with the coming of a new minister. Given the same people, the same social environment, the same instruments to work with, one man will discover to the church its real reason for being and uncap latent forces of great spiritual power while the other will fail."[13]

There are a number of ways to list the varied aspects of pastoral leadership. In *Overseers of the Flock,* Dr.

[11]H. B. Trecker, quoted by W. Curry Mavis, *Advancing the Smaller Local Church* (Winona Lake, Ind.: Light and Life Press, 1957), p. 88.

[12]Leonard Mayo; quoted by Mavis, *loc. cit.*

[13]Quoted by Trueblood, *op. cit.,* pp. 35-36.

G. B. Williamson lists six guiding principles: (1) The delegation of responsibility, in which the pastor is flexible enough to work with all kinds of people; (2) The enlistment of cooperation; (3) The attitude of magnanimity, largeness of spirit, and sympathy; (4) The keeping of a sound financial policy; (5) Emphasis on fundamentals, and (6) Maintaining a vital spiritual program.[14]

Dr. Curry Mavis points out that pastoral leadership must be both strong and democratic—that it must avoid two opposite dangers: (1) the *laissez-faire* attitude, abdicating the responsibility for positive leadership; and (2) the autocratic attitude, ignoring the need for democratic process. Such leadership, Mavis concludes, involves as prime qualifications in the pastor: vision for growth; ability to challenge the acceptance of responsibility; ability to recognize and deal with personal tensions; and resources of confidence, optimism, and courage.[15]

One author has written: "A congregation of people want in their midst a man who can lead them into the reality of worship, who can inspire them with brave, clean and moving preaching, who can teach them the relationship between life and religion, who can counsel them in regard to their personal problems and comfort them in their sorrow, and who can administer the business affairs of the parish with dispatch. Notice the verbs involved in this list of qualifications: lead, inspire, teach, counsel, comfort and administer. These are the functions of the ministry."[16]

[14] (Kansas City: Beacon Hill Press, 1952), pp. 171-78.

[15] *Op. cit.*, p. 88.

[16] "Blueprint for a Seminary," *Religion in Life*, Winter, 1946-47, p. 211.

Leaving the more general summaries, let us note some of the functions, ideals, and attitudes involved in the minister's role as overseer.

IV

There is always the very obvious need for strong leadership in financing the work of the church. If anyone ever objects to the raising of an offering, he could well be cited to II Corinthians 8—9, where Paul devotes two chapters to one offering.

Church economics will always have something about it of the character of "frenzied finance" as long as we back into it—drawing up our spending budget first, and then setting out to find the money. Unfortunately, money is always easier to spend than it is to get.

The pastor must see to it that designated funds are always handled with the most scrupulous care. Church funds are all trust funds and must be treated as such.

While the pastor will be responsible ultimately for the finances of the church, he should always seek to work through his strongest lay group. He should never personally be involved in collecting or disbursing funds, except as an emergency matter. Even then he should never accept money without giving a receipt, and should never spend money without getting a receipt. In all cases, he must make a scrupulous and immediate accounting.

Even the smallest church could well have a finance committee, although its work would probably never be presented as was done by one pastor who in explaining the function of the committee said, "You know, the pastor is the shepherd of the flock; and the finance committee acts as his crook."[17]

[17]Quoted in *Together*, January, 1961.

The pastor's own finances are of utmost importance. He may find himself faced with the necessity of living and looking like a professional man on less than the income of a day laborer. But unless his income equals his outgo, his upkeep will be his downfall! It is rightly said that there are two sins God may forgive but people never will: looseness in relations with the opposite sex, and carelessness in handling money.

V

A less tangible but vitally important area in pastoral administration is building sound morale in the church. Most "problem churches" are afflicted with low morale. It is true that the morale may be affected by some "built-in" problems for which there is no apparent solution. But low morale may also be the cause of problems which in their turn serve to intensify the spirit of discouragement and defeat.

Curry Mavis points out that past failures, small size, lower economic-social status, and personality tensions all serve as hindrances to morale. The pastor in building morale must find ways to inspire enthusiasm, recognize merit in others by giving appreciation as freely as possible, and by helping to reduce tensions through his own understanding of people.[18]

However, no objective problem causes morale to collapse more quickly and more completely than a discouraged leader. Discouragement is a contagion that spreads faster than measles in a country school. And the minister is even more exposed to discouragement with the progress of his church than others. His is the highest vision of what ought to be. And he experi-

[18]*Op. cit.*, p. 4.

ences most sharply the devastating contrast with what is. One who expects nothing experiences no particular disappointment when nothing happens. To expect much and see little can very quickly lead to deep discouragement.

Most of us have probably found Elijah under the juniper tree wishing to be out from under it all, and have more than once nudged him and said, "Move over, Elijah, and make room for me." But we must learn, with Elijah, God's remedy for low moods.

Two phases of the Lord's cure for His prophet's deep discouragement were fellowship and the challenge of renewed activities and tasks. Both are important. Any place of leadership is often a lonely spot. Like all others, the pastor needs the fellowship of peers. Herein is the value of ministerial prayer cells, fellowship breakfasts or luncheons, or associations of various sorts. Then, the vigorous pursuit of other tasks has great therapeutic value in the face of temptation to the "blues."

But one of the most important aspects of God's remedy for Elijah's low mood was rest and food and care for his physical body. He slept and was fed. In terms of our day, this may mean a vacation. It always means proper recreation. There are always those who argue that the devil never takes a vacation—"So why should I?" I would simply ask, "Since when is the Christian minister to pattern his life after the devil?" Jesus urged His disciples to "come ye yourselves apart into a desert place, and rest a while" (Mark 6:31). The fact that the rest was interrupted does not change the intention thus revealed.

The ministry is subject to actual physical hazards in the form of hypertension, heart disease, nervous exhaustion, and not infrequently, ulcers. Paul's statement at Lystra, "We also are men of like passions with you"

(Acts 14:15), has more than one application. Wayne Clark warns his ministerial brethren that "neglected Sabbaths collect compound interest after the age of forty."

Dr. Daniel Blain, himself a minister's son and for years medical director of the American Pyschiatric Association, has written:

> The minister will seek to establish an adequate program of recreation, refreshment, and replenishment which will serve to restore his energies and nourish his mind and spirit. One of the basic elements in such a program is to secure sufficient rest and relaxation through sleep, taking naps, or simply loafing. High creativity seems to depend upon these fallow periods, and new insights and inspiration often come during or just after such quiet times. Periods of prayer and meditation may serve the same purpose if they are relaxed rather than tense, if they are periods of waiting rather than worrying. Another aspect of such a program is to rest the much-used parts of the organismic structure by activating other parts. So a change of activity or occupation may in itself be restful. Fortunately, the ministry usually entails a wide variety of activities so that it often has a kind of built-in recuperation.[19]

Most of us have heard the legend of the Early Church in which the aged Apostle John is pictured as going out occasionally to play with a flock of doves. The birds would flutter about and alight on his hands and shoulders while he talked with them as if they were human friends. One day, it is said, a hunter who happened along expressed surprise that one so devout as St. John would amuse himself in such a trivial activity. John pointed to the bow in the hunter's hand and asked him why he carried it with the bowstring loosened.

[19]In Oates, *The Minister's Own Mental Health*, pp. 29-30.

"Because," said the other, "it loses its strength unless it is given a chance to unbend."

John, smiling, replied, "If even a piece of wood needs to unbend to retain its usefulness, why should you be surprised that a servant of Christ should sometimes relax and so keep himself stronger for his work?"[20]

A pastor who had suffered and recovered from a complete nervous breakdown wrote anonymously to his fellow ministers in the *Christian Advocate*:

> It might be well for us to ask ourselves if we are trying too hard. We are important, for surely God works through persons. When he sought to reveal his complete nature and redeem the world he did it through a Person. And he is doing it through us.
>
> It is important for us to remember, however, that God is still God. It may be that we have been trying to be God, that we have taken ourselves so seriously that we have felt it necessary to labor beyond our strength, and with strain, rather than to go about our tasks with the calm confidence that, having given ourselves and our talents to him, his must be the victory.
>
> We must always remember that playing is almost as important as praying. We ought to be able to play without a sense of guilt.
>
> I have always despised a lazy preacher. But there is certainly a need for finding wise recreational activities that rest the body and the mind because they are different from the general round of ministerial activities.
>
> Let us beware of fatigue. Dr. Edgar Spencer Cowles of the Body-Mind Clinic in New York wrote that he had never known a case of depression that did not begin with fatigue. When it is difficult to sleep, and when we find it hard to laugh, we ought to take warning.[21]

[20]Retold by Paul S. Rees, *Prayer and Life's Highest* (Grand Rapids: Wm. B. Eerdmans Publishing Co., 1956), pp. 42-43.

[21]December 20, 1962, p. 15.

From an entirely different context and yet entirely relevant to the ministry come the words of Winston Churchill in his book *Painting as Pastime*:

> To be really happy and really safe, one ought to have at least two or three hobbies, and they must be real. Change is the master key. A man can wear out a particular part of his mind by continually using it and tiring it, just the same way as he can wear out the elbows of his coat. There is, however, this difference between the living cells of the brain and the inanimate articles; one cannot mend the frayed elbows of a coat by rubbing the sleeves or shoulders; but the tired parts of the mind can be rested and strengthened, not merely by rest, but by using other parts. It is not enough merely to switch off the lights which play upon the main and ordinary field of interest; a new field of interest must be illuminated. It is no use saying to the tired "mental muscles"—if one may coin such an expression—"I will give you a good rest," "I will go for a long walk," or, "I will lie down and think of nothing." The mind keeps busy just the same. If it has been weighing and measuring, it goes on weighing and measuring. If it has been worrying, it goes on worrying. It is only when new cells are called into activity, when new stars become the lords of the ascendent, that relief, repose, refreshment are afforded.[22]

VI

The pastor as overseer must also combine flexibility in methods with fidelity to the message of the church. Whatever else it may include, the command of Jesus to His disciples recorded in Luke 22:35-36 indicates the changing methods required by changing circumstances: "And he said unto them, When I sent you without purse, and scrip, and shoes, lacked ye any thing? And they said, Nothing. Then said he unto them, *But now,* he that hath a purse, let him take it, and likewise his

[22]Quoted by Ralph Turnbull, *op. cit.*, pp. 119-20.

scrip: and he that hath no sword, let him sell his garment, and buy one" (*italics mine*).

Dr. J. B. Chapman expressed this in a classic chapter printed in *Heart Talks with Ministers,* edited by E. E. Shelhamer. Entitling his discussion "The Unchanging Message and the Changing Methods," Dr. Chapman said:

> The essential message of the gospel is the same in all ages, but the method of presenting it requires adaptation to times and conditions.
>
> Perhaps we all feel that there is something which is stable and something which is transient. But if we get confused and make the stable transient and the transient stable we are headed for disaster.
>
> The modernist, for example enamored with the idea of change and adaptation, scruples not to adapt the essential message and in so doing robs the gospel of its power and exposes his own soul to the consequences of damning doubt.
>
> But there is another man who is impressed with the thought of the unchanging and he applies this quality to methods as well as to the message and he becomes a moss-back, a back number and a failure. He may save his own soul, but he will not be able to save the souls of others, because he is incapable of becoming "all things to all men" even in matters that are only incidental. . . .
>
> Thirty years ago [this was written in the 1920's] all that seemed to be needed was a preaching place. But now the Sunday school, young people's work and various other legitimate and useful departments must be housed and provided with equipment as necessities, and not merely as luxuries. But we have a tendency of becoming attached to what "used to be" in these incidental matters and then we refuse to move away from them and accuse those who want to move as being compromisers.
>
> But the very most serious thing of all is the demand for adaptation on the part of the preacher himself along with his passing years and changing conditions. It is the habit of old men to dream dreams, whereas the progress of the work of God depends upon the prophets

who can see visions. It is never possible to lead back to "what used to be." Movements must always be, in a sense, on into fields which have never yet been explored.

Some preachers have done better the first decade of their ministry than they ever do later. Up to that time they were teachable and adaptable, then they began to quote precedents and to rely upon "experience" and they died of hardening of the arteries.

It is only a step beyond success to where success becomes a danger and pitfall. A man can usually succeed better with a little success behind him, but it takes a great man to succeed with a great deal of success behind him. This is not because success is within itself a liability, but it is because the average man who succeeds will not change his methods with the changing times, and in the course of time, he who was once "ahead of his times" is so far out of date that he is more valuable for a museum than for anything else.

Here is the unchanging message, "Jesus Christ the same yesterday, and to day, and for ever." Here are the limits to which one may go in changing the methods of propagating the message: "I am made all things to all men, that I might by all means save some.[23]

We must never confuse doggedness with devotion, or think of all change as compromise. Compromise does involve change, but so do growth and progress. Loyalty to the church of the nineteenth century or even to the church of the 1930's may be treason to the church of the twentieth century or of the 1960's and 1970's. Living organisms survive as they grow and adapt themselves to meet new demands. Rigidity is one of the signs of death.

Churches and their leaders are basically conservative in their attitudes. Mullen comments, "It should not

[23]Reprinted in the *Herald of Holiness,* LVI, No. 14 (May 24, 1967), 9.

be surprising to ministers that it was a preacher who wrote in Ecclesiastes:

> *What has been is what will be,*
> *and what has been done is what will be done;*
> *and there is nothing new under the sun.*
>
> —Eccl. 1:9 (RSV)"[24]

Leonard Chafin notes along this line also, "Institutions tend to preserve the best of the past. For this we can be thankful. They also tend to become intimidated by change. The church has adopted so much of the spirit of the day that radical change is unthinkable. In the modern church the cardinal sin can be 'rocking the boat.' The goal of many pastors is to keep things going smoothly. The dedicated member is one who 'cooperates.' This is hardly the atmosphere in which the re-thinking of the mission of the church is apt to take place."[25]

The solution to the problems we encounter in the area of adapting methods to changing circumstances lies in maintaining what Paul called "a sense of what is vital" (Phil. 1:10, Moffatt). We must have a clear understanding of the essentials and the incidentals of our most holy faith, and a clear distinction between them. Dr. R. T. Williams used to comment that he would most hate to choke to death on a piece of ice. He would always think that if he could just have held on a little longer the ice would have melted. The ultimate ministerial tragedy is to suffer martyrdom for something which really doesn't matter very much anyway.

[24]*Op. cit.*, p. 128.

[25]*Help! I'm a Layman* (Waco, Tex.: Word Books, 1966), p. 87.

VII

Pastoral leadership also demands the capacity to work closely and harmoniously with the lay officials of the church. The minister always faces the possibility that his congregation may not elect those he wants as members of the board. In fact, the pastor is headed for serious trouble who tries to "handpick" his board. As little as we may like it, opposition is generally good for us. It keeps us on our toes, for one thing. The supreme test of both character and leadership can be the way one meets opposition.

Layman Leonard Spangenberg, somewhat with tongue in cheek, gives a "Recipe for a Typical Church Board": "Take one or two old-timers, add a son or daughter, tag on a 'know it all,' salt down with a maiden lady, stir it up with a one-track-minded grammar school graduate, then put them all in a small room and you have a fairly good sample of a church board."[26]

The need here is for magnanimity and patience. The pastor must not identify his plans and desires with the eternal will of God. He must avoid what has been bluntly labeled a "God-complex." Peter warns those who have oversight of the flock of God not to set themselves up as "little tin gods" (I Pet. 5:3, Phillips). D. T. Niles recalls that his second son, when a child, said, "Papa, I want to be a preacher when I grow up." His father asked him why. They were standing in the church where Niles was then pastor. The lad pointed up to the pulpit and said, "I want to stand inside that and tell everybody what they must do."[27] Rather volumi-

[26]*Minding Your Church's Business* (Kansas City: Beacon Hill Press, 1942), p. 16.

[27]Paul S. Rees, *Triumphant in Trouble* (Westwood, N.J.: Fleming H. Revell Co., 1962), p. 127.

nous correspondence from lay people across the past nine years convinces me that such an attitude is not altogether unknown among us.

The pastor must cultivate empathy with the leaders of the local church—even when he encounters a "church boss." The layman does have a distinctive point of view, and his pastor needs to recognize and appreciate it. He may not always be wrong. After all, the layman has seen pastors come and pastors go, but he pays on—it seems like forever!

The pastor may indeed know better than his laymen what ought to be done. But he would be smart to wait until they see it too. Spangenberg notes: "The wise pastor usually gets what he wants but only after a majority want it. He does not quibble over small matters nor does he railroad things through. In a calm and thoughtful manner he presents all sides of a case. . . . His 'I want this' and 'I insist upon that' are portrayed in such a way as to bring about co-operation, not opposition."[28]

VIII

The pastor-leader must see to it that an effective lay organization is developed within the church. He must remember that it is far better to get 10 men to work than to do the work of 10 men. The prime function of every administrator is the selecting and training of a staff. The most searching test of administrative effectiveness is to leave a strong and undivided church to one's successor.

Dr. Williamson writes: "The pastor who does not know how to delegate responsibility will soon find himself with so much tinkering to do that he has no time

[28]*Op. cit.*, p. 17.

to spend in the things with which he should be primarily concerned. Instead of being big, he is small, because he is always doing small things. Instead of being an executive, he is an errand boy."[29]

It is important that the church utilize the increasing leisure time of its laymen. Purposive and productive activity raises morale quicker than any other factor. The ideal should be, "A task for every man, and a man for every task." Especially is this important in churches with high standards of Christian life and conduct to help offset the danger of introspective, subjective piety at the expense of a full-orbed spiritual life. The church which does not organize for outreach will often turn in upon itself.

To persuade qualified people to accept responsibility, and to train good leaders to become better, is a never ending task. There can be real value in a "personnel committee," with a program of active training of prospective leaders and in-service training of those presently in office. Too many offices for one person represents weakness rather than strength. And too long in the same office may also be bad. It isn't always a compliment to have served 25 years as Sunday school superintendent. It may just mean that it has taken that long to get the man out. Twenty-five years in an office doesn't always mean 25 years of experience. It may just mean one year's experience repeated 25 times.

IX

It should go without saying that the overseer of the flock must keep the spiritual goals of the church constantly in mind. All effective administration must be

[29] *Op. cit.*, p. 173.

judged in the light of the objectives of the organization. We must remember that the God we serve weighs as well as counts. Our work must be evaluated qualitatively as well as quantitatively. This must never be taken as basis for the rationalization of smallness. Yet it is true that "they who live by statistics shall perish by statistics."

The pastor's own attitudes in his administrative work must be in harmony with the ultimate goals of his ministry. A single display of impatience or unreasonableness in a tense board meeting can undo the effects of months of tearful preaching. The pastor must himself be an example of all he preaches. A man may be crooked and be a good attorney. He may be sick and be a good doctor. But he cannot be insincere or unspiritual and be a good pastor. John Knox of Union Theological Seminary in New York has somewhere written, "When I think of those who have influenced my life the most, I find that it is not the gifted but the good." And Francis Pigou is quoted as saying, "More men are won to God by holiness than by cleverness."

The overseer must avoid as the plague itself the tendency to become afflicted with what Dr. L. J. Du Bois has fittingly called "administrivia." It is possible to ease the pain of failure in the real essentials by the "anesthesia of activity."[30] J. H. Jowett long ago said, "We are not always doing the most business when we seem to be the most busy. We may think we are truly busy when we are really only restless, and a little studied retirement would greatly enrich our returns. We are great only as we are God-possessed."[31]

Not all the busyness of the modern minister is thrust

[30]The phrase coined by Gene Bartlett, *op. cit.*, p. 131.
[31]Quoted by Turnbull, *op. cit.*, p. 102.

upon him. Much of it is assumed by him. Kyle Haselden said, "In far more cases than would admit it, the minister is over-burdened because he wants to be over-burdened. He wears many hats in church and community because the multiple roles they represent constitute his only identity, his image of himself. This man's name is Legion; his sense of integrity is dependent not upon his being one thing but precisely upon his being many things. His ministry is a 'shish kebab' and the more items of activity and responsibility he can add to his skewer, the less he worries about the absence of the main course."[32]

And Bartlett, again, challenges us to consider, "in all honesty, how much of our activity, so often decried by those who want to keep reality in the ministry, is imposed and how much is chosen? To what degree are we impelled from within and to what degree are we compelled from without? Here some moments of searching honesty are required of us. For an impressive portion of our activity seems self-chosen. In the face of the fundamental alarm, it is in some ways flight to an easier alternative. For it *is* easier to promote than to pray. It *is* easier to be in one's office than in the study. It often *is* easier to serve on a committee than to face the question of one's real commitment. It may be difficult to raise a budget, but it is infinitely more difficult to raise a spirit which has been crushed by the circumstances of life, or by the relentless inner tensions which bind men."[33]

We have already quoted extensively from Dr. J. B. Chapman in this chapter. But I would like to close with his "Charge to Ministers": "I charge you to keep

[32]*The Urgency of Preaching*, p. 110; quoted, Stevenson, *op. cit.*, p. 100.

[33]*Op. cit.*, pp. 131-32.

your hearts alive in the things of God. Be men of prayer and faith, and do not be satisfied with anything short of a continuous sense of the divine presence in your hearts and lives. If you find your spiritual tide running low, call yourselves to prayer and fasting and to humbling yourselves privately before God until He shall pour out His Spirit upon you anew. This will enable you to preach with unction and power and will give you an element in your work that cannot be described in terms of human force and power. Insist on praying through to God every day and allow nothing to take the place of this divine assurance. Be clean and holy in your lives. Abstain from all appearance of evil. God help you as ministers of the Gospel to remember this charge."[34]

[34]Quoted without notation of source in a district preachers' meeting program.

Bibliography

BOOKS

ARNOLD, MILO L. *The Adventure of the Christian Ministry.* Kansas City, Mo.: Beacon Hill Press of Kansas City, 1967.

AUTREY, C. E. *The Theology of Evangelism.* Nashville: Broadman Press, 1966.

BARCLAY, WILLIAM. *Corinthians.* "The Daily Bible Study." Philadelphia: The Westminster Press, 1956.

———. *The Epistle to the Hebrews.* "The Daily Bible Study." Philadelphia: The Westminster Press, 1955.

———. *Fishers of Men.* Philadelphia: The Westminster Press, 1966.

———. *The Letter to the Romans.* "The Daily Bible Study." Philadelphia: The Westminster Press, 1957.

———. *The Mind of Saint Paul.* New York: Harper and Brothers, 1958.

———. *The Promise of the Spirit.* Philadelphia: The Westminster Press, 1960.

BARTH, KARL. *Prayer and Preaching.* Naperville, Ill.: SCM Book Club, 1964.

BARTLETT, GENE E. *The Audacity of Preaching.* The Lyman Beecher Lectures. New York: Harper and Brothers, 1962.

BLACKWOOD, ANDREW W. *Special-Day Sermons for Evangelicals.* Great Neck, N.Y.: Channel Press, Inc., 1961.

———. *The Fine Art of Preaching.* New York: The Macmillan Co., 1937.

BOULDING, KENNETH E. *The Image: Knowledge in Life and Society.* Ann Arbor: The University of Michigan Press, 1956.

BOWERS, GEORGE K. *God Here and Now.* Anderson, Ind.: The Warner Press, 1961.

BROADUS, JOHN. *The Preparation and Delivery of Sermons.* New York: Harper and Brothers, 1926.

BROMILEY, G. W. *Christian Ministry.* Grand Rapids, Mich.: Wm. B. Eerdmans Publishing Co., 1959.

BUTLER, G. PAUL, ed. *Best Sermons*: Vol. IX, 1964, Protestant Edition. Princeton, N.J.: D. Van Nostrand Company, Inc., 1964.

CHAFIN, KENNETH. *Help! I'm a Layman.* Waco, Tex.: Word Books, 1966.

CHAMBERS, OSWALD. *The Moral Foundations of Life.* Third Edition. London: Marshall, Morgan and Scott, Ltd., 1962.

CLARKE, JAMES W. *Dynamic Preaching.* Westwood, N.J.: Fleming H. Revell, 1960.

CLIFFORD, PAUL ROWNTREE. *The Pastoral Calling.* Great Neck, N.Y.: Channel Press, 1961.

CUNNINGHAM, ROBERT B., ed. *Behold a New Thing.* Department of Evangelism, United Presbyterian Church in the U.S.A., n.d.

CUSHMAN, RALPH SPAULDING. *The Essentials of Evangelism.* Nashville: General Board of Evangelism, The Methodist Church, 1946.

DAVIES, D. R. *On to Orthodoxy.* New York: The Macmillan Co., 1949.

DAVIES, HORTON. *A Mirror of the Ministry in Modern Novels.* New York: Oxford University Press, 1959.

DAVIS, HENRY GRADY. *Design for Preaching.* Philadelphia: Fortress Press, 1958.

EICHRODT, WALTHER. *Theology of the Old Testament.* Volume I. Translated by J. A. BAKER. Philadelphia: The Westminster Press, 1961.

ELLIOTT, WILLIAM M., JR. *Power to Master Life.* The Message of Philippians for Today. New York: Abingdon Press, 1964.

FARMER, HERBERT H. *The Servant of the Word.* New York: Charles Scribner's Sons, 1942.

FISHER, WILLIAM. *Evangelistic Moods, Methods, and Messages.* Kansas City, Mo.: The Beacon Hill Press of Kansas City, 1967.

FORD, LEIGHTON. *The Christian Persuader.* New York: Harper and Row, 1966.

FORSYTH, P. T. *Positive Preaching and the Modern Mind.* New York: George H. Doran Company, 1907.

———. *The Soul of Prayer.* Grand Rapids, Mich.: Wm. B. Eerdmans Publishing Co., reprint of 1916 publication.

GEIGER, KENNETH, compiler. *Further Insights into Holiness.* Kansas City, Mo.: The Beacon Hill Press of Kansas City, 1963.

GREEVES, FREDERIC. *Theology and the Cure of Souls.* An Introduction to Pastoral Theology. Manhasset, N.Y.: Channel Press, Inc., 1962.

HANSON, ANTHONY T. *The Church of the Servant.* Naperville, Ill.: SCM Book Club, 1962.

HAVNER, VANCE. *Pepper 'n Salt.* Westwood, N.J.: Fleming H. Revell Company, 1966.

HENRY, CARL F. H., ed. *Contemporary Evangelical Thought.* Great Neck, N.Y.: Channel Press, 1957.

HORDERN, WILLIAM. *New Directions in Theology Today.* Vol. I, Introduction. Philadelphia: The Westminster Press, 1966.

JONES, E. STANLEY. *Growing Spiritually.* New York: Abingdon Press, 1953.

KEIR, THOMAS H. *The Word in Worship.* London: Oxford University Press, 1962.

KEMP, CHARLES F. *Pastoral Preaching.* St. Louis, Mo.: The Bethany Press, 1963.

KENNEDY, GERALD. *For Preachers and Other Sinners.* New York: Harper and Row, 1964.

———. *Fresh Every Morning.* New York: Harper and Row, 1966.

KENNEDY, JAMES. *Minister's Shop-Talk.* New York: Harper and Row, 1965.

KENT, HOMER A., SR. *The Pastor and His Work.* Chicago: The Moody Press, 1963.

KOHLER, LUDWIG. *Old Testament Theology.* Translated by A. S. TODD. Philadelphia: The Westminster Press, 1957.

MACARTNEY, CLARENCE E. *Autobiography: The Making of a Minister.* Edited and with an introduction by J. CLYDE HENRY. Great Neck, N.Y.: Channel Press, Inc., 1961.

MALTZ, MAXWELL. *Psycho-Cybernetics.* New York: Prentice-Hall, 1960.

MAVIS, W. CURRY. *Advancing the Smaller Local Church.* Winona Lake, Ind.: Light and Life Press, 1957.

MINEAR, PAUL S. *Images of the Church in the New Testament.* Philadelphia: The Westminster Press, 1960.

MOUNCE, ROBERT H. *The Essential Nature of New Testament Preaching.* Grand Rapids: Wm. B. Eerdmans Publishing Co., 1960.

MULLEN, THOMAS J. *The Renewal of the Ministry.* New York: Abingdon Press, 1963.

NEILL, STEPHEN, ed. *Twentieth Century Christianity.* Dolphin Books; Garden City, N.Y.: Doubleday and Co., Inc., 1963.

NILES, DANIEL T. *The Preacher's Task and the Stone of Stumbling.* New York: Harper and Brothers, 1958.

OATES, WAYNE E. *Protestant Pastoral Counseling.* Philadelphia: The Westminster Press, 1962.

———, ed. *The Minister's Own Mental Health.* Great Neck, N.Y.: Channel Press, Inc., 1961.

PEARSON, ROY. *The Ministry of Preaching.* New York: Harper and Brothers, 1959.

PELIKAN, JAROSLAV. *The Christian Intellectual.* New York: Harper and Row, 1965.

REES, PAUL S. *Prayer and Life's Highest.* Grand Rapids: Wm. B. Eerdmans Publishing Co., 1956.

———. *Stir Up the Gift.* Grand Rapids: Zondervan Publishing House, 1952.

———. *Triumphant in Trouble.* Westwood, N.J.: Fleming H. Revell Co., 1962.

RICHARDSON, ALAN. *An Introduction to the Theology of the New Testament.* New York: Harper and Brothers, 1959.

ROWLEY, H. H. *The Faith of Israel*: Aspects of Old Testament Thought. Philadelphia: The Westminster Press, 1956.

SANGSTER, W. E. *The Approach to Preaching.* Philadelphia: The Westminster Press, 1953.

SCHERER, PAUL. *The Word God Sent.* New York: Harper and Row, 1965.

SCHROEDER, FREDERICK W. *Preaching the Word with Authority.* Philadelphia: The Westminster Press, 1954.

SITTLER, JOSEPH. *The Ecology of Faith.* Philadelphia: Muhlenberg Press, 1961.

SMITH, GEORGE ADAM. "Isaiah, Vol. I." *The Speaker's Bible,* edited by EDWARD HASTINGS. Aberdeen, Scotland: "The Speaker's Bible" Office, 1934.

SMITH, ROY L. *The Future Is upon Us.* New York: Abingdon Press, 1962.

STEVENSON, DWIGHT E. *The False Prophet.* New York: Abingdon Press, 1965.

STEWART, ALEXANDER. *The Shock of Revelation.* New York: The Seabury Press, 1967.

STEWART, JAMES S. *Heralds of God.* New York: Charles Scribner's Sons, 1946.

STOTT, JOHN R. W. *The Preacher's Portrait*: Some New Testament Word Studies. Grand Rapids, Mich.: Wm. B. Eerdmans Publishing Company, 1961.

TAYLOR, J. PAUL. *Holiness, the Finished Foundation.* Winona Lake, Ind.: Light and Life Press, 1963.

THIELICKE, HELMUT. *Encounter with Spurgeon.* Philadelphia: Fortress Press, 1963.

THIESSEN, JOHN CALDWELL. *Pastoring the Smaller Church.* Grand Rapids: Zondervan Publishing House, 1962.

TIZARD, LESLIE J. *Preaching: The Art of Communication.* New York: Oxford University Press, 1959.

TOOMBS, LAWRENCE E. *The Old Testament in Christian Preaching.* Philadelphia: The Westminster Press, 1961.

TOZER, A. W. *Man, the Dwelling Place of God.* Harrisburg, Pa.: Christian Publications, Inc., 1966.

TRUEBLOOD, D. ELTON. *The Incendiary Fellowship.* New York: Harper and Row, 1967.

TURNBULL, RALPH G. *A Minister's Obstacles.* Revised. Westwood, N.J.: Fleming H. Revell, 1946.

VALENTINE, FOY. *The Cross in the Marketplace.* Waco, Tex.: Word Books, 1966.

VINE, W. E. *An Expository Dictionary of New Testament Words.* Four volumes. London: Oliphants, Ltd., 1940.

VRIEZEN, TH. C. *An Outline of Old Testament Theology.* Boston, Mass.: Charles T. Branford Company, 1958.

WATSON, PHILIP S. *The Message of the Wesleys.* A Reader of Instruction and Devotion. New York: The Macmillan Co., 1964.

WEATHERSPOON, JESSE BURTON. *Sent Forth to Preach.* Studies in Apostolic Preaching. New York: Harper and Brothers, 1954.

WHITESELL, FARIS D. *Power in Expository Preaching.* Westwood, N.J.: Fleming H. Revell, 1963.

WILLIAMS, DANIEL DAY. *The Minister and the Care of Souls.* New York: Harper and Brothers, 1961.

WILLIAMS, HOWARD. *Down to Earth*: An Interpretation of Christ. Naperville, Ill.: SCM Book Club, 1964.

WILLIAMSON, G. B. *Overseers of the Flock.* Kansas City, Mo.: Beacon Hill Press of Kansas City, 1952.

YATES, KYLE M. *Preaching from the Prophets.* New York: Harper and Brothers, 1942.

ARTICLES

CHAPMAN, J. B. "The Unchanging Message and the Changing Methods." *Herald of Holiness,* Vol. LVI, No. 14 (May 24, 1967), reprint.

DAVISON, J. A. "Rehabilitating the Sermon." *Church Management,* Vol. XLII, No. 9 (June, 1966).

GARRISON, CLAUDE. "Fresh out of Boot Camp." *Christian Advocate,* Sept. 13, 1962.

KEMP, CHARLES F. "On the Work of the Pastor." *The Christian,* Vol. C, No. 47 (Nov. 25, 1962).

KENNEDY, GERALD. "We Never Had It So Good." *Pulpit Digest,* Vol. XL, No. 261 (Jan., 1960).

LUCCOCK, HALFORD. "Simeon Stylites." *Christian Century,* Vol. LXXVII, No. 11 (March 16, 1960).

MACLEOD, DONALD. "The Creative Preacher." *Bulletin of Crozer Theological Seminary* (April, 1962).

MOSER, CHARLES E. "Portrait of a Minister." *Pulpit Digest,* June, 1962.